DISCOVERING SOCIOLOGY

Edited by Peter Langley

AUTHORS

Steve Chapman
Julia Fiehn
Hugh Chignell
Shaun Best
Peter Langley
Patrick McNeill
Martin Slattery
Ian Marsh
Carol Hayden
Roger Gomm
Rob Pattman

Causeway Press

INTRODUCTION

In recent years the task of teachers and students of 'A' level Sociology has been eased by the appearance of various general and topic based textbooks. However, there remains a lack of books which encourage students to develop their own 'sociological imaginations' through active involvement in evaluating evidence and drawing conclusions. *Discovering Sociology* aims to fill this gap.

Discovering Sociology rests on the assumption that all kinds of everyday material such as photographs, cartoons and newspaper articles can be used to make sociological points. Also, that sociology is not a subject which can be neatly divided into discrete topics. Most chapters in *Discovering Sociology* cross traditional topic boundaries in order to link relevant issues. Rob Pattman's chapter on AIDS, for instance, focuses on the 'moral panic' surrounding AIDS in order to make points about the media, deviance, race and gender. The book also attempts to demonstrate the relevance of sociology to understanding contemporary issues: the Labour Party's current dilemmas are put into context in both 'Why do the Conservatives keep winning General Elections' and 'The Working Class', while the chapter on 'Community' should provoke thought on the current crisis in the inner cities.

All of the above points have been emphasised in recent examiners' reports. Moreover, the proposed new structure for one AEB 'A' level paper requires students to demonstrate exactly those skills that they should develop in using *Discovering Sociology*.

The book can be used in a variety of ways. Students can work through chapters on their own, using the activities to check and develop their understanding. Teachers can go through chapters in class and/or set various activities as homework. When the book is used in the classroom it is suggested that many activities are particularly appropriate as group work tasks. Students should be encouraged to question the reliability of sources, even though this may not be built into specific activities.

Discovering Sociology makes no attempt to cover the entire syllabus. Instead, it focuses on a number of controversial and examinable issues. It is hoped that there will be further volumes of *Discovering Sociology*. If you are interested in contributing to a further edition, please send your ideas to me at Causeway Press.

Finally, I would like to thank Sally Holmes, Theresa McCoy and, particularly, Hugh Chignell for their help during the final stages of editing. I should also like to thank Roger Gomm for the inspiration for this book.

Peter Langley
Editor, *Discovering Sociology*

Causeway Press Limited
PO Box 13, Ormskirk, Lancs. L39 5HP
©Causeway Press Limited 1988
1st Impression 1988

British Library Cataloguing in Publication Data

Discovering sociology.
 1: Sociology
 I. Langley, Peter, 1954–
 301

 ISBN 0–946183–42–2

Typesetting by Chapterhouse, Formby.
Printed and bound by The Alden Press, Oxford.

CONTENTS

Acknowledgements

Written and graphical material

The authors and publishers are grateful to all those who permitted the use of copyright material in this book. Due acknowledgement has been made to each source in the text. Data from *Social Trends* and OPCS reproduced with the permission of the Controller of Her Majesty's Stationery Office, Crown copyright reserved.

Photographs and cartoons

Associated Press pp. 9, 14 (middle), 36 (bottom left and right), 61 (top right), 66, 67 (top right), 70 (bottom), 71, 72, 96 (bottom), 104
Brick pp. 50 (top and bottom), 53
Bristol United Press Ltd pp. 61 (top left), 81
Brooke Bond Oxo Ltd p. 1
Central TV pp. 2, 54
Granada TV p. 25
Guardian Newspapers p. 26
Ingrid Wright pp. 30 (bottom), 67 (top right)
Library of Congress p. 18 (right)
London Weekend Television Ltd p. 46
Mansell Collection pp. 16, 45, 78 (top left)
Mary Evans Picture Library pp. 10, 18 (left), 22, 75, 78 (top right), 96 (top)
McDonald's Hamburgers Ltd p. 46
Network pp. 30 (top), 32, 41 (left), 48 (left), 60, 61 (bottom left)
Oxfam p. 48 (right)
Pete Addis p. 68 (top)
Posy Simmonds p. 4

Press Association p. 41 (right)
Punch pp. 15, 79 (left)
Red Rose Radio p. 68 (bottom)
Rex Features pp. 44, 74, 84
Sally & Richard Greenhill pp. 70 (top), 82
Socialist Worker/Phil Evans pp. 61 (bottom right), 62
Steve Bell p. 99
Times Newspapers p. 6
Whitbread plc p. 15 (right)
Windridge and Jane p. 63
Yorkshire Art Circus Ltd p. 27

Original artwork

Howard Prescott, The Art Factory, Lytham pp. 29, 33, 47, 49, 52, 55, 56, 58, 59, 67, 86, 87, 93, 95

Original cartoons

Jill Richardson p. 57
Roger Gomm p. 92
Val Biro pp. 36, 51, 69, 91

Cover design

Windridge and Jane

Every effort has been made to locate the copyright owners of material included. Any omissions brought to the publisher's notice are regretted and will be credited in subsequent printings.

UNIT 1　The Family: Ideology and Reality

A certain type of family and family interaction is presented as the ideal in Great Britain by various social agencies. This unit poses two related problems: (a) What is this ideal? and (b) How does it correspond with reality?

Introduction

It is important to understand when we examine the family that we are dealing with an institution with which most of us are familiar. We spend a great part of our lives in families. The family is very much a cornerstone of our taken-for-granted world. It is not surprising, therefore, that many of us should claim to be experts in family life and what it should ideally entail. Consequently the commonsense notions derived from our experiences are part of the debate about the role of the family in modern society. However this unit aims to examine the idea that some individuals and groups have the power to dominate that debate and thus define for the rest of us an ideal type of family structure and behaviour. In other words, does an ideology or dominant set of beliefs and ideas exist about family life which permeates our own family experience? Clearly if such an ideology exists it is important that as sociologists we should attempt to stand aside from such family experiences. We should not assume that our experience is the norm. As the Bergers [1976] argue, 'We need to introduce a sufficient element of artificial strangeness into what is most familiar to us in order that we may describe the familiar in clearer ways.'

It is useful when exploring the concept of the family to begin with an examination of media images of family life. It is argued by Liberal Pluralists that the mass media in all their varied forms reflect social reality. They transmit images and representations of family life that are shared by everyone.

ACTIVITY 1

Examine the photograph opposite. This is an advertising agency's image of a typical British family. Using this and other media output with which you are familiar e.g. commercials, soap operas and situation comedies, construct a detailed model of the media's 'ideal family'. You should employ the following concepts; careers, class, leisure, lifestyle, race, social relationships, sex roles, size and structure.

1.1

A shot from an Oxo commercial

Tolson notes that the mass media especially the tabloid press concentrate on what he terms '**the cult of the royal family**'. Barrett and McIntosh (1982) note that it is not the institution of monarchy that is popular but the vision of family life that the royal family is seen to symbolise.

ACTIVITY 2

(a) What 'vision of family life' do you think is symbolised by the royal family?

(b) How does extract 1.2 confirm the importance of the royal family to British family life?

(c) What issues may the concentration on 'royal family' rather than 'monarchy' distract us from?

1.2

FAMILIES – even Royal ones – have a way of growing on you. Almost before you notice.

In 1947, when the Queen married, you could have driven a ceremonial coach and horses through the Royal family as they stood on the Palace balcony.

Today, as she and Prince Philip celebrate their Ruby Wedding, you can barely see the balcony floor for Royal relatives.

What started in 1947 as almost an intimate family snapshot, begins now to resemble something cast by Cecil B. de Mille.

It must appear as if they all crept in while Her Majesty's back was turned.

But the Royals, with every addition, represent for us all the strength of family life. And for the Queen, surely, it must reflect the success of her own marriage and her reign.

The contented look she and Prince Philip display on such occasions gives us the hint. They are, after all, playing their favourite game, *Happy families*...

Source: *Daily Mirror* 20.11.87

Barrett and McIntosh argue that mass media representations of family life are aspects of the **ideology of familism**; a set of ideas and images relating to family structure and relationships which dominates debate about how family life ought to be lived in Britain. It is noted by Gittins (1985) that an attribute of familism is the notion that there is crisis in the family. Social problems are seen to be the direct result of a decline in family values. Smith (1986) refers to commentators who take this position as **neo-traditionalists**. He says that they 'are against permissiveness in sexual behaviour, against pornography, against feminism, against liberal methods in education and sometimes against abortion'. Neo-traditionalists therefore are in favour of a return to '**traditional**' values. Extracts 1.3 and 1.4 are typical of this position.

ACTIVITY 3

(a) **List** the social problems and deviant activities mentioned in the extracts associated with the breakdown of family life. What other current concerns might you add to this list?

(b) Describe the type of family life you think Johnson (1.3) and Gale (1.4) envisage as the ideal.

(c) What social trends inside and outside the family are said to have resulted in the 'weakness of family life'?

(d) What solutions do you think Johnson and Gale might offer to arrest the 'decline of the family'?

1.3

LAST WEEK, in a major three part series, Paul Johnson, right wing journalist and ideologue, laid out a proposed agenda for a third Conservative term of office in the leader pages of the Daily Telegraph. He devoted the whole first part to The Family and called upon the Conservatives to become the standard bearers for family life and traditional moral values.

In his usual powerful polemical style, Paul Johnson spells out the problem. "The breakdown of family life is a huge social and economic, as well as moral, evil. The foot-soldiers in every inner city riot are those who have never known a proper home...A child deprived of a normal family life is far less likely to grow up educated, employable and law-abiding. The weakness of family life in Britain is most probably the biggest single cause, not merely of habitual crime, but also of poor educational standards and so of chronic unemployment. All these evils are interconnected. The financial and economic cost is incalculable. The cost in human misery doesn't bear thinking about."

Johnson accuses the left of deliberately undermining family life, with its approval of gays, its promotion of contraception (and hence promiscuity) in sex education.

Source: *Guardian* 12.1.85

1.4

Miss Diamond—not a girl's best friend

ANNE Diamond, the bubbly girl of Breakfast Television, the giggly girl next door, the ordinary girl who does an extraordinary job extraordinarily well, is to become an unmarried mother.

The mind sighs and the heart sinks.

She and her lover, recently divorced Mike Hollingsworth, are apparently committed enough to each other to have a child, but 'not committed enough to marry'.

We need not look on them too severely, for their fundamentally irresponsible and selfish attitude is all too characteristic of the times we live in.

"Now I want to be a family person" she said. "And I feel a family programme, with a lady presenter in the family way is quite a nice idea."

Sure

Is it? Are families rejecting marriage true families at all? Is a pregnant presenter with no intention of getting married all that nice for a family programme?

Miss Diamond can afford her child. As soon as she has had it she will be back at work paying other women to look after it.

She may be a good mother. She will never be a burden on the community as most unmarried mothers are.

But her example will encourage other girls to become unmarried mothers and other couples to forego the commitment of getting married.

And so she does her bit to wreck the institution of marriage, the family's only sure foundation.

It is a pity, even a kind of tragedy. The girl next door is about to become the unmarried mother next door.

We lost our innocence years ago, when the girl next door ceased to be a virgin. Now, we are losing our sense of responsibility as well, a much greater loss.

Source: *Daily Mirror* 1986 (article by George Gale)

There is a good deal of evidence which suggests that the neo-traditionalist view of the family is supported by the Government and its agencies.

Recently Margaret Thatcher has expressed fears about the threat to family life which she describes as that 'little bit of heaven on earth' whilst Kenneth Baker, the Education Secretary plans to ensure that sex education in schools is taught within a new moral framework emphasising commitment, love and the value of family life. (*The Guardian*, 6.6.86)

The Posy Simmonds cartoon (1.6) succinctly summarises this official position.

Patricia Allatt (1.5) argues that governments of all political persuasions in Britain have contributed to the construction of familistic ideology. She notes that familism is made up of stereotypical assumptions about the role of men and women in the family. Such assumptions have become institutionalised in law and social policy despite the fact they do not reflect the reality of everyday experience for a great number of families.

ACTIVITY 4

(a) Identify *four* stereotypical assumptions made about family life in the cartoon.

(b) What 'omissions' (see first paragraph, 1.5) have been made in the construction of these stereotypes?

(c) Apply Allatt's arguments (1.5) to the following official regulations and policy decisions. What family stereotypes are being encouraged?
1) Different retirement ages for males and females.
2) The invalid care allowance is available to everyone (except married or co-habiting women) who care for a disabled person for at least 35 hours a week and who have little or no income from savings.
3) The married man's tax allowance. No such allowance is available to co-habiting men or co-habiting/married women.
4) The right to unemployment benefit depends upon 'availability to work'. Women with young children are not regarded as eligible for such benefit.
5) Social security payments to women are dependent upon the 'co-habitation' rule. If it is established that the woman is living with a man, it is automatically assumed that they are together as man and wife, and benefit to the woman is immediately stopped.
6) In 1977 council day nurseries and playgroups, nursery schools and classes altogether provided about 162,000 places for a total pre-school population of 3 million.

1.5

Gender stereotypes

The selective interpretation of reality is a characteristic attributed to stereotypes . . . while based in real behaviour stereotypes distort by omission, that is, they select only part from the total complexity of an individual's daily experience. Reality is splintered . . .

Legal material . . . provides numerous instances of constraining regulations which correlate with identifiable stereotypes . . . For example, the protective legislation of the Factory Acts and the earlier retirement age of women lend support to the stereotype of the weaker sex despite biological evidence to the contrary witnessed in the greater longevity of women. Women do not work at night (unless engaged in occupational domestic work such as nursing or office cleaning) and few women remain in the workforce beyond 60 years of age. Presumed innate gender differences in conceptual thinking find a place in the existing tax system which is based on the legal premise that a wife's income, for tax purposes, is 'deemed' to belong to her husband. The head of the household cannot enact his role as citizen and fill in his tax forms unless his wife tells him how much she earns. Numerous tax and social welfare regulations sustain the stereotype of the male breadwinner.

Source: P. Allatt, 'Stereotyping: Familism in the Law', in Fryer *et al, Law, State and Society*, (Croom Helm 1981)

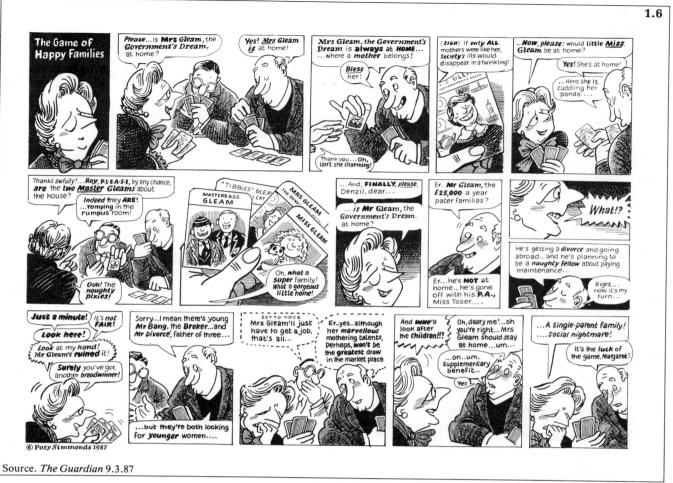

Source. *The Guardian* 9.3.87

Central to the ideology of familism are certain assumptions about **motherhood**. These can be seen in the work of the anthropologists Tiger and Fox (1974) who argue that motherhood is biologically programmed. They note that 'nature intended mother and child to be together'. Similarly the child psychologist John Bowlby has argued that if children are deprived of maternal love for prolonged periods of time they may grow up to be psychologically disturbed.

ACTIVITY 5

(a) Which character in the play (1.7) would support the sentiments of Tiger and Fox and John Bowlby? List the statements that she makes which justify your choice.

(b) How does extract 1.4 from George Gale support the views of John Bowlby? Which group do Gale and Bowlby hold responsible for social and family problems?

(c) What would be the political, economic and social implications of discovering that fatherhood was just as important for the psychological development of children as motherhood?

(d) Why do you think there have been few studies of fatherhood?

(e) What effects might theories such as maternal deprivation have on women's occupational ambitions?

1.7

Motherhood and fatherhood

Stella: What kind of set-up is this? What is it when we're all clucking about like hens with our Lucozade and knitting and sticking our bloody bums in the air? Can you see a man doing that?

Fran: Are you saying you think men ought to have more to do with their families? Because if that's what you mean you don't know them. Have you seen men with babies? It's laughable. I think it's a crime to leave a child with a man.

Caroline: Come off it, Fran.

Stella: That's just crap.

Fran: Is it? I'm sorry. I wouldn't go out to work and leave Heidi with Graeme. I wouldn't trust him. They push prams – have you watched them? You'd think they were walking on nails. His idea of playing with Heidi is to sit her in the nursery and watch her through a newspaper. That's why it's a woman's job. Because men can't do it.

Stella: You mean WON'T do it.

Fran: No, it's just not in them with all the will in the world. A child goes to it's mother. You don't have to tell it.

Stella: What do you expect? Your husband isn't wearing milk bottles, is he?

Fran: No, he isn't. And I don't think that's an accident.

Caroline: You sound like you've learned it by rote, Fran. I am a woman. I have a uterus. I bear fruit. And meanwhile, Man hunts. Drags the kill home. Provides.

Fran: Because it's always been like that doesn't make it wrong. Just unfashionable.

Stella: Just bollocks.

Caroline: I don't think you believe it. But if you say it often enough you can live with it.

Fran: No! I'm sick and tired of women telling me I'm wasting my life. Envy thy husband's penis. No, I'm sorry. You have to cut it off now, don't you? There is something that neither of you can understand. You talk about love, Stella – you've no idea – because it's not love with men and women, it's necessity. Love is between the mother and her child. That's why you're so poisoned. That's why men work so hard at making everying else look more fulfilling, because it's not their magic, it's my magic. And what's so sad, so terribly shabby, is that women are abandoning what they have because they think men are hiding some miracle in their hands. But there's no miracle . . .

Source: *Whale Music* by Anthony Minghella

Our exploration of family ideology has resulted in a very clear picture of what family structure and relationships ought ideally to be like. Most people think of the typical British family in terms of a married couple with children relatively isolated from kin. Sociological research, especially that of Wilmott and Young, suggests that this nuclear family is the norm today. We now need to examine the empirical evidence to assess the extent of this family type.

ACTIVITY 6

(a) Examine the table *Households: by type* (1.8)
  (i) What percentage of households live in families in 1985?
  (ii) What percentage of family households live in nuclear units?
  (iii) What trends in household type can be perceived between 1961 and 1985?
  (iv) What types of family structure other than the nuclear unit are suggested by the statistics?

(b) Examine the table *Households and people in households: 1981* (1.9)
  (i) Robert Chester (1985) argues that household statistics are only a 'snapshot' of family life and, are therefore, misleading. What evidence in this table supports this view?
  (ii) Which family structure is normal and still experienced by the great majority?
  (iii) How might the family life cycle change the structure of other family types?

1.8

Households: by type

	1961	1971	1976	1981	1984	1985
			Percentages			
No family						
One person						
Under retirement age	4	6	6	8	9	9
Over retirement age	7	12	15	14	16	15
Two or more people						
One or more over retirement age	3	2	2	2	2	1
All under retirement age	2	2	1	3	2	2
One family						
Married couple only	26	27	27	26	26	27
Married couple with 1 or 2 dependent children	30	26	26	25	24	24
Married couple with 3 or more dependent children	8	9	8	6	5	5
Married couple with independent child(ren) only	10	8	7	8	8	8
Lone parent with at least 1 dependent child	2	3	4	5	4	4
Lone parent with independent child(ren) only	4	4	4	4	4	4
Two or more families	3	1	1	1	1	1
Total households	100	100	100	100	100	100

Source: *Social Trends*, HMSO, London, 1987

1.9

Households and people in households. 1981

type of households	% of households	% of people
one person	22	8
married couple	26	20
married couple with dependent children	32	49
married couple with independent children	8	10
lone parent with dependent children	4	5
other	9	8

Source: 'The Rise of the Neo-Conventional Family' by Robert Chester, *New Society*, 9.5.85.

It would seem from the statistical evidence that the ideology of familism has some support in terms of family structure. Nuclear families do not make up the majority of households but the majority of people will live in nuclear units at some stage in their lives. However it can be argued that our beliefs about the value of the nuclear unit may lead to problems for those not living in this family type. In other words the ideology of familism may have negative consequences for some groups.

Working class Asian families are one such group whose family type may not conform to the nuclear ideal.

ACTIVITY 7

(a) What type of family structure is suggested by the photograph and family tree?

(b) What expectations and supports are generated by this type of family?

(c) In what ways do these traditional supports and expectations clash with dominant beliefs about family life in Britain?

(d) What do you think is the future for such family units?

(d) Asians are not the only group in Britain to find this type of family network useful. What other groups are likely to maintain such networks?

Karam Chand lived and worked in Britain alone for ten years before his wife and children could join him from the Punjab. Though he knew living in Wolverhampton would mean changes for them all, it never seriously occurred to him that they might have to revise their notion of family life . . . Karam Chand's old home in India remains a benchmark for his family life in Wolverhampton. The household that lived in the roomy accommodation around the courtyard included his parents and his unmarried sisters, his own family and also those of his two younger brothers.

'The family', to an Asian extended family takes in all these people. A special relationship exists between father and son. Those who are dependent upon father or son are included on their account. Within their family there is not merely a common house-keeping arrangement but totally shared financial responsibility.

Tradition carries penalties. Neither tax relief nor income based benefits like rate rebates are geared to extended family financial systems. Karam Chand and his sons are almost certainly losing financially. But they would not consider trying to do anything about this. It is a matter of principle. Karam Chand sees the financial loss as a small price to pay for keeping the extended communal concept intact.

Source: adapted from 'How far do family ties go – the Indian answer' by Jane Morton, *The Times*, 12.5.82

1.10

NOT FAMILY	FAMILY 1	FAMILY 2
Families of sons' wives (Help in emergency)	Direct male line including son's wives & unmarried daughters	Families of married daughters (Help in need, clan wide enterprises)

UHDI (56)		KARAM CHAND (65) CHINT KAUR (59)				
MANOHAR HIRA (13)	SAT NAM (24) KAUSHALIA DEVI	SAT PAL (28) SASO PAL	KRISHANDA (19)	RESHAM KAUR (32) + husband	JOGINDER DEVI (25) + husband	
		RAKESH PAL (14 months)		Children	Children	

Despite the popularity of the nuclear unit there is some evidence that family structure may be changing. The number of one parent families has doubled since 1961. In 1987 it was estimated by the Study Commission on the Family that one child in seven – one child in three in the inner city – was living in this type of family. However as we have seen the ideology of familism is made up of values about 'normal' family life. Popay *et al.* (1.12) argue that one parent families represent 'an obvious and visible challenge to many of these values and formal and informal attitudes to such families, reflecting this, are often ambiguous and sometimes actually unsympathetic'. Take, for example, the assertion that one parent families are 'evil' made by Dr. Rhodes Boyson, a Conservative minister in October 1986.

ACTIVITY 8

(a) Give three reasons why one parent families may come about.

(b) Why is the risk of poverty greater for one parent families than nuclear families?

(c) What are the implications of material deprivation for health, education and general adjustment?

(d) Why might the neo-traditionalist view of the family perceive one parent families as evil?

(e) What contradictions can you see in the neo-traditionalist attitudes to parenthood?

(f) Most one parent families are female headed. In the light of previous extracts what institutional bias might such families face?

(g) How might negative stereotypes and labels about one parent families held by professional workers result in:
   (i) educational failure
   (ii) over-representation of children from broken homes in the delinquency statistics?

1.11

OPINION
The growing problem of single parents

NOT everyone will relish the bluntness with which Environment Minister Dr Rhodes Boyson expresses his concern about one-parent families, particularly those he calls "intentional".

Many, however, will share that concern. Because, between 1971 and 1981, the number of one-parent families grew by 71 per cent. It is still growing.

One in eight families is now one-parent. One in seven children comes from such a home, and in inner cities the proportion can rise to one in three or four.

The damaging impact of this new social phenomenon on the children themselves and society at large is truly alarming.

We all know well-adjusted children brought up by just one parent, usually the mother. Some women have the emotional, physical and financial resources to bring them up successfully without the aid of a husband.

The father image

These children and these mothers, alas, are not the norm, as countless studies show.

Though some pressure groups seek to deny or ignore the evidence, it is overwhelming. It shows that children from single-parent families are *more likely* to have problems—and cause problems—at school, and to be delinquent.

Boys in particular have been found to suffer from having no father, or stable father figure, around the house.

Dr Boyson, who was headmaster of an inner-city comprehensive before entering politics, says such boys can only be "civilised" by firm and caring fathers. Without an adult male figure to look up to at home, too many teenage boys tend to get their ideas of proper masculine behaviour from members of their gang, and that behaviour is likely to be aggressive and lawless.

Of course, the presence of two parents is no guarantee that children will turn out well. It is still a far better bet than the presence of just one.

Dr Boyson worries that the prevalence of "intentional" one-parent families will spread. Certainly, there are going to be more broken homes, as the latest divorce statistics depressingly indicate.

If his fears are not to be borne out we need to return to traditional standards of self-discipline and personal responsibility.

Above all, we need a return to the recognition that an enduring relationship within marriage is the best basis for rearing a child.

Source: *Daily Express*, October 1986

1.12

Perceptions of one parent families

On the basis of recent research it is possible that more than one third of low income families are headed by a lone parent. The risk of poverty for these family units is very much greater than for two parent families and the extent of poverty is likely to be much more extreme.

Social workers, teachers, health visitors ... may come into contact with parents and children from one parent families which means their perceptions of such families may be a vitally important influence on their practice. Whilst it cannot be denied that there may be special circumstances to which such professionals need to be sensitive it may be that the absence of a parent per se is itself viewed as problematic. The family circumstances will therefore be seen as inevitably negative, regardless of other circumstances.

... Bias can be introduced into an analysis of links between family circumstances and delinquency which is based on children in care and custody. Children from family backgrounds which are considered 'abnormal' may be more likely to be taken into custody than children from 'normal' homes even when similar offences are involved.

Source: *One Parent Families: Parents, Children and Public Policy* by J. Popay, L. Rimmer and C. Rossiter, Study Commission on the Family, 1983

It is argued by Oakley (1974) that familistic ideology may have negative consequences for women. For example, she argues that 'the myth of maternal deprivation' has operated to make employed mothers feel guilty and inadequate. She contends that familistic ideas about motherhood are designed to keep women in the home. Both Oakley and Ginsberg (1976) argue that the result for many women is loneliness and boredom. Oakley notes that the monotony of housework and the social isolation of being housebound leads to a sense of alienation and in some cases, clinical depression.

ACTIVITY 9

(a) Examine data 1.13. How does the experience of being a housewife compare with the experience of working in a factory or on an assembly line?

(b) What problems for married women are suggested by Tax (1.14) and Griffin (1.15)?

1.13

The experience of monotony, fragmentation and speed in work: housewives and factory workers compared.

Workers	percentage experiencing		
	Monotony	Fragmentation	Speed
Housewives	75	90	50
Factory Workers	41	70	31
Assembly line workers	67	86	36

Source: adapted from *Housewife* by Ann Oakley, Penguin, 1974

1.14

'I am nothing by myself'

When I am by myself, I am nothing. I only know that I exist because I am needed by someone who is real, my husband and by my children. My husband goes out into the real world. Other people recognise him as real and take him into account. He affects other people and events. He does things and changes things which are different afterwards. I stay in his imaginary world in this house doing jobs that I largely invent and that no-one cares about but myself. I do not change things. The work I do changes nothing; what I cook disappears, what I clean one day must be cleaned again the next. I seem to be involved in some sort of mysterious process rather than actions that have results.

The only time that I think I might be real is when I hear myself screaming or having hysterics. But it is at these times that I am in most danger... of being told that I am wrong or that I'm not really like what I'm acting like or that he hates me. If he stops loving me, I'm sunk; I won't have any purpose in life or be sure I exist anymore. I must efface myself in order to avoid this and not make any demands upon him or do anything that might offend him. I feel dead now but if he stops loving me I am really dead because I am nothing by myself. I have to be noticed to know that I exist. But if I efface myself how can I be noticed?

Source. Meredith Tax, 'Woman and Her Mind; The Story of Daily Life' 1970, quoted in S. Rowbotham, *Woman's Consciousness, Man's World*, Penguin, 1973

1.15

Voices by Susan Griffin

They call me Grace,
Yesterday I went
to the grocery store
I had filled up
the cart
and was halfway through
the check stand
before I realised
I had shopped for the whole
family.
The last child left
two years ago
I don't know what
got into
me.
I was too embarrassed
to take the things back
so I spent the week cooking
casseroles.
I feel like one of those
eternal motion machines

designed for an
obsolete task
that just keeps on
running.
I certainly don't want them
back either
When the
last baby stopped getting
up at
night I didn't stop...
...And William never
understood. To him
if you are tired, you sleep,
I have never been able to
penetrate the
simplicity of his logic
which is
after all
the logic
of most of the world

Source *Half the Sky*, The Bristol Women's Study Group, Virago, 1979

The ideology of familism presents us with a very positive picture of family life. The 'cornflake family' appears to suffer no problems. Family members interact happily with each other. In recent years this rosy picture has come under attack. It has been suggested that the public image of the nuclear family may mask severe problems which may result in physical and mental harm to its members. Burchill (1.16) argues that institutional practices such as social work are informed by familistic ideology which stresses the need to keep the family together. She maintains that the imposition of family life on people unsuited to it creates the major social problems of our society.

R.D. Laing, a radical psychiatrist (1.17), argues that the intensity of some family interaction may result in schizophrenia for some members.

ACTIVITY 10

(a) How does the argument of Burchill (1.16) compare with that of the neo-traditionalists in extracts 1.3 and 1.4?

(b) Examine the symbolism used in the Laing extract (1.17).
  (i) Who are the players?
  (ii) Think carefully about the way the ball is used. Suggest family situations which can be used to illustrate Jane's experiences.

(c) Edmund Leach (1971) suggests that the problems which Burchill and Laing identify occur because the domestic household is isolated from kin and neighbours. 'The family looks inward upon itself.' Explain what he means by this.

(d) How does the concept of the stereotypical happy family make these problems difficult to detect?

1.17

Schizophrenia and the family

Jane was absorbed in a reverie of a perpetual game of tennis. Mixed doubles. Centre Court. Wimbledon. The crowd, the court, the net, the players, and the ball, back and forth, back and forth, back and forth. She was all these elements, especially the ball.

   This ball was served, smashed, volleyed, lobbed, sometimes hit right out of court – so small, so passive, yet so resilient – the centre of the game and the spectacle. All eyes are on it. Though resilient, its endurance is limited. It can be worn out, though it began with a lot of bounce. It is the medium of the relationship between the players. They apply spin, trick and cheat with it. Although it is so essential, no one is really interested in it. They use it or want it only to beat the other side. Sometimes they treat it gently but only to win. No one cares about it. It is treated entirely ruthlessly. If the ball should protest or rebel, or not keep up with the beating it is taking, if it aspires to initiative, or option how to bounce, where go to, it will be thrown away. The game's the thing: not perhaps even fundamentally a matter of winning it, but of perpetuating it.

Source: *The Politics of the Family* by R.D. Laing, Penguin, 1976

1.16

The last sacred cow

As the sixties swung to a standstill, in the final summer, the golden girl film actress, Sharon Tate, and a handful of house guests were butchered in a Hollywood bungalow. The killers, it transpired, were a murderous, paranoid unit who called themselves the Family. At the time, the name seemed a surprising choice.

   In the light of recent headlines, it makes perfect sense. What better name for a murderous, paranoid unit than the FAMILY? Of all recorded murders, the majority take place within the family. Of all recorded assaults, the majority take place within the family. Of all recorded child abuse, sexual or otherwise, the majority take place within the family. Some reports suggest that one in 20 girls is a victim of incest, a quarter under the age of five. One child a week in Britain dies at the hands of its parents, usually its father, starved, suffocated, punched to death. Reported cases of child abuse within families have gone up 70% in six years.

. . . a good three-quarters of violence is domestic, from punching a wife to killing a child. Taking this into consideration, it is not the breakdown of family life that causes violence – but the endless promotion and protection of what goes on within it.

Source: 'The Last Sacred Cow' by J. Burchill, *New Society*, 27.12.85

Charles Manson, leader of 'The Family' after his arrest in Los Angeles, 1970

Burchill notes that of all recorded assaults the majority take place within the family. Rebecca and Russell Dobash (1.18) examined police and court records for a period of a year in Edinburgh and Glasgow relating to family violence. They argue that marital violence is seriously under-estimated in the statistics. Furthermore social and institutional responses to domestic violence are only understandable in the light of familism which stresses the private rights and freedoms of the family unit. Thus what goes on within the family is regarded by society as a private affair. However Dobash and Dobash conclude that the beneficiaries of such an ideology are men and as such familistic ideology is patriarchal.

ACTIVITY 11

(a) According to the statistics which family member is in greatest danger of physical injury?

(b) Why may these statistics be under-estimated?

(c) What is the institutional response to such violence according to Pizzey (1.19)?

(d) Why do you think the police are reluctant to intervene in and prosecute such violence?

(e) How might social attitudes towards the role of women in marriage and one parent families influence a wife's response to domestic violence?

(f) What other forms of patriarchal dominance and control are suggested by previous extracts?

(g) Judging from the drawing (1.20), what was seen as a major cause of domestic violence in the last century? In your opinion, what are the main causes of marital violence today?

1.18

Types of assault occuring between family members, Edinburgh and Glasgow, 1974

Person attacked	No.	Percentage
Wife	791	75.8
Husband	12	1.1
Child	112	10.7
Parent	73	7.0
Sibling	50	4.8
Mutual	6	0.6
Total	1,044	100.0

The use of physical violence against women in their position as wives is not the only means by which they are controlled and oppressed but it is one of the most brutal and explicit expressions of patriarchal domination. The position of women and men as wives and husbands has been historically structured as a hierarchy in which men possessed and controlled women.

Patriarchal domination through force is still supported by a moral order which reinforces the marital hierarchy and makes it very difficult for a woman to struggle against this, and other forms of domination and control, because her struggle is construed as wrong, immoral and a violation of the respect and loyalty a wife is supposed to give to her husband.

Source: *Violence Against Wives* by R. Dobash and R.E. Dobash, Open Books, 1979

1.19

Scream quietly!

The police attitude to wife battering reveals an understandable but unacceptable schizophrenia in their approach to violence. Imagine that Constable Upright is on his beat one night and finds Mr Batter mugging a woman in the street. Mr Batter has already inflicted heavy bruises to the woman's face and is just putting the boot in when Constable Upright comes on the scene. The constable knows his duty and does it. He arrests Mr Batter, who is charged with causing bodily harm and goes to prison for ten years.

Ten years later Constable Upright is on his beat when he is sent to investigate screaming which neighbours have reported coming from the home of the newly released Mr Batter. Mr Batter is mugging his wife. He's thrown boiling water at her, broken her nose, and now he's trying for her toes with a claw hammer. When Constable Upright arrives what does he do? Does he make an arrest? Of course not.

He knocks on the door and Mr Batter tells him to 'sod off'. He tells Mr Batter that the neighbours are complaining and he wishes to see his wife. Mr Batter says they have been having a minor row and gets his wife who is looking bruised around the face and crying. The policeman will not arrest.

Source: *Scream Quietly or the Neighbours Will Hear* by Erin Pizzey, If Books, 1974

1.20

'The Bottle' – drawing by nineteenth century artist George Cruikshank

---

Both feminist and Marxist sociologists have linked the emergence of the nuclear family and familistic ideology to industrialisation. Oakley (1.23) and Gittins (1.21) argue that industrialisation resulted in the promotion of patriarchal ideas such as familism which ensured the power of men over women in the spheres of work and home. Marxist feminists such as Hartmann (1.22) argue that familistic ideology supports and legitimates capitalist social relations. As a result familism is a dominant set of beliefs. Alternative ideas which challenge the nuclear family norm are suppressed or defined as deviant by ideological apparatuses such as the government and the law. Familism in this sense is hegemonic – an integral part of ruling class ideology.

ACTIVITY 12

(a) According to Gittins (1.21) and Hartmann (1.22), why has the role of housewife come about?

(b) How has science contributed to the legitimation of familistic ideology?

(c) What personal service work does the housewife perform? How might such work contribute to the smooth running of capitalist society?

(d) How might a family wage actually weaken the power of working class men?

(e) Give *two* examples of 'men feeling powerful and being powerful' in families which may have negative consequences for women. How might such power compensate for the social organisation of the workplace for some men?

(f) How might familism divide the working class?

(g) Family ideology is patriarchal. In the light of *all* the evidence presented in this chapter, how true to you think this statement is?

(h) What modifications do you think Hartmann (1.22) would make to that statement?

1.21
Capitalism and the family

The ideology of the family... is an historical creation. The very concept of family was not used in the way it is today until the late eighteenth century. Its development as a concept and an ideology was an inherent part of the development of the industrial bourgeoisie during the later stages of capitalist development.

From the seventeenth century onwards, the development of science... perpetuated fundamental beliefs about authority and gender.

Men were seen as 'naturally' authorative, stronger, more intelligent, and women were 'naturally' deferential, weak, passive and intuitive. Men, therefore, were suited to govern, to make decisions, to direct women and children, and these patriarchal assumptions became an integral part of science, of the ways in which governments and government policies were perceived and formulated.

Source. D. Gittins, *The Family in Question*, Macmillan, 1985

1.22
Patriarchy

The material base of patriarchy is men's control over women's labour power. That control is maintained by excluding women from access to necessary economically productive resources and by restricting women's sexuality. Men exercise their control in receiving personal service work from women, in not having to do housework or rear children, in having access to women's bodies for sex, and in feeling powerful and being powerful. The crucial elements of patriarchy as we currently experience them are; heterosexual marriage (and consequently homophobia), female child rearing and housework, women's economic dependence on men (enforced by arrangements in the labour market), the state...

We argue that patriarchy as a system of relations between men and women exists in capitalism and that in capitalist society a healthy and strong relationship exists between patriarchy and capital....Instead of fighting for equal wages for men and women, male workers (in the nineteenth century) sought the family wage, wanting to retain their wives' services at home...patriarchal social relations divided the working class, allowing one part (men) to be bought off at the expense of the other (women).

Source: H. Hartmann, *The Unhappy Marriage of Marxism and Feminism: Towards a more progressive union*, Pluto Press, 1981

1.23
The housewife role

The most important and enduring consequence of industrialization for women has been the emergence of the modern role of housewife as 'the dominant mature feminine role'.

Source *Housewife* by Ann Oakley, Penguin, 1974

Conclusion

It is clear that a dominant set of ideas and beliefs, an ideology, about how family life ought to be lived, exists in our society. These ideas are transmitted through such agencies as the mass media and government departments, and are apparent in political and academic debate. However it is evident in contemporary Britain that such an ideology in presenting the nuclear family and certain family values, roles and relationships as 'ideal' devalues other family systems, and conceals and disguises the tensions and strains of nuclear family life. The consequences for some family members especially women can be dire. The ideology of the family, therefore, may do more harm than good. As Gittins (1985) argues 'an ideology that claims that there is only one type of family can never be matched in reality, for it presents an ideal to which only some can approximate, and others not at all. It is this attribute of family ideology which makes people believe there is a crisis in the family while the real problem is the gap between ideology and reality.' (p. 167)

Further reading

Bristol Women's Studies Group *Half the Sky*, Virago, 1979
Gittins, Diana *The Family in Question*, Macmillan, 1985
Oakley, Ann *Subject Women*, Fontana, 1981
Popay, Jenny *et al. One Parent Families: Parents, Children and Public Policy*, Study Commission on the Family, 1983
Segal, Lynne *What is to be done about the Family*, Penguin, 1983

UNIT 2   Childhood

In this unit we are going to look at the following questions. How has the concept of 'childhood' developed in Britain? What are the reasons for the apparent contradictions between the image and reality of childhood?

Introduction

Everyone experiences childhood and most of us would agree that what happens to us in our early years has an enormous influence on the way we later develop and perceive the world. The influences on children are different depending on the society they live in and its view of what children *are* and what they *need*. Even within one society, different social groups may be treated differently. For example, girls and boys have very different experiences of childhood, and there are variations in child care between social classes. The way children are treated can tell us a great deal about a society or groups within a society. It is particularly interesting to look at the contradictions between what people say about childhood and what happens to some children. The two extracts on the following page illustrate one of the contradictions between image and reality.

A.   The image of childhood

ACTIVITY 1

(a) What image of children is common in Britain today?
Using sources 2.1 and 2.2, list words and phrases that are regularly used to describe a child.

(b) What techniques are used in these two sources to reinforce the image?

(c) Suggest reasons why, in the light of this image, child abuse as reported in the newspaper article (2.3) is regarded as particularly shocking.

2.1

For a BOY Who's 3

2.2

"Well, everyone needs a little security."

The Playskool Blankies are made for hugging. And squeezing. And holding tight.

There's calf and piglet, lamb and lion cub, baby giraffe and elephant. Once your baby has learned to love one, they'll never be apart. (They're the smartest security blankets ever.)

Each little pet has a soft blanket body and embroidered eyes.

So they're safe in your baby's hands or mouth. (The blanket body is non-toxic and machine washable too.)

And while you're secure in this knowledge, your baby can enjoy the comfort and security of a lovable, huggable Blankie.

THE PLAYSKOOL BLANKIES

Sharing in the magic of the PLAYSKOOL years.

2.3

Child abuse figures increase by 22 pc

By Martin Wainwright

A national survey of the number of children registered by local authorities as in danger of abuse shows a sharp increase of 22 per cent, rising by more than 30 per cent in parts of the country.

The figures, collated by the Association of Directors of Social Services, were circulated to its principal officers yesterday. Figures are also given for sharp rises for those children considered in danger specifically of sexual abuse.

The Association of Directors of Social Services' figures are based on questionnaires returned by 100 councils. They show a sudden rise in 1985–86 in the number of children regis-

tered as at risk, an increase similar to that in a sample taken by the NSPCC.

The national average increase of 22 per cent was exceeded in London (30 per cent), Yorkshire and Humberside (36 per cent) and several other regions.

For children considered in danger specifically of sexual abuse, two councils reported than an increase from four to 42 cases from 1980 to the end of 1985 had leapt by 95 in 1985–86.

The report suggests that the rise is largely due to increased awareness of the problem by both social services and the public.

Source: *Guardian* 7.7.87

It is a feature of twentieth century parenthood that advice on child care is frequently sought by the new parent, and such advice is freely available in books such as Jolly's (2.4), quoted here. This extract represents the opinion of the 'expert'.

Childhood has become the area of the paediatrician – a separate medical specialisation in which not only the medical but also the psychological needs of the child are seen as important.

ACTIVITY 2

(a)   What reasons does Jolly (2.4) give for his view that child care should be the subject of study for all parents?

(b)   How have ideas about children changed, according to him, thanks to 'expert' opinion?

2.4

vital in laying down the individual's future pattern, both as regards whether he achieves his full intellectual potential and whether he is sufficiently secure and well rounded as a personality. Since these early years are so vital is there any need to argue the need for child upbringing to be a subject of study, in books and other media, for all parents?

The modern mother takes for granted that she will have the advice of experts and will not have to rely on the advice of her mother. The previous generation of mothers may not necessarily be the best advisers of the present generation. This is not to belittle the enormous support which grandmothers can give—it is, indeed, unfortunate that this support is less easily obtained because today's married daughters are less likely to live near their parents. But the modern mother is less convinced than her predecessors that her mother knows best. At the same time the 'experts' should not be regarded as infallible; it is up to you to be selective about the balance between other people's advice, whether relatives or experts, and decide how it applies to your own individual baby.

Today's parents are probably better at bringing up their children than any previous generation. They are more aware of the importance of the early years and, knowing this, they are more concerned not to make mistakes.

Child care

I am often asked whether I think it is a good idea for parents to read books on child care and for there to be radio and television programmes on the subject. As the author of this book I have obviously answered in the affirmative—but why?

Before answering the question it is relevant first to ask why it comes to be asked. We accept that training and advice are required for every job a man or woman undertakes. The job of bringing up our children, the most important we undertake, is no exception.

Fortunately, most of us bring to this task the in-built expertise given by our parents in the way they handled us as children. If we were 'mothered' well by our parents we have at least a head start on those whose intellect is the same but whose childhood experiences were less happy. The early years of life are the most

Source: *Book of Child Care* Hugh Jolly, George Allen & Unwin 1975, pp. 17–18

Childhood is seen as a time in a person's life entirely distinct from all other times, when the individual has different needs, interests and outlook.

Throughout the last 150 years, legal protection of children has increased, covering many aspects of life.

ACTIVITY 3

(a) Some of the legislation affecting young people under the age of 18 is given in extract 2.5. List all the aspects of life in which young people are required by law to be protected or controlled, (eg work, sex etc.).

(b) The cartoon (source 2.7) suggests that the expectations adults have of young people can be confusing.
What contradictions exist in these expectations?
Use source 2.5 to give examples.

(c) Compare the expectations of young people in this country with what is shown in the photograph of Iranian girls (source 2.6).

2.6

Source: cartoon by J. Nesbitt in *Childhood* by Y. Beecham, J. Fiehn and J. Gates, Harrap/Nelson, London, 1980

2.5

From birth
You can have an account in your name with a bank or a building society
You can have premium bonds in your name
You can have a passport of your own (if one of your parents signs the application form)

At age 5
You can drink alcohol legally in private

At age 7
You can draw money from a post office or savings account

At age 10
You can be convicted of a criminal offence if it is proved that you knew the difference between right and wrong

At age 12
You can buy a pet animal

At age 13
You can be employed for a certain number of hours a week

At age 14
You can be held fully responsible for a crime
You can be fingerprinted if you are in custody and charged
You can be convicted of a sexual offence (applies to boys only)
You can pawn an article in a pawn shop
You can go into a pub, but not drink or buy alcohol there

At age 15
You can see a '15' film
You can be sent to Borstal
You can be sent to prison to await trial (applies to boys only)

At age 16
You can buy premium bonds
You can sell scrap metal
You can buy cigarettes or tobacco
You can join a trade union
You can leave school
You can choose your own doctor
You can claim social security benefit
You can work full-time

You can have sexual intercourse (applies to girls only: if a girl under sixteen has sexual intercourse, her partner, the boy, is liable to prosecution)
You can leave home with your parents' consent
You can get married with one parent's consent
You can drink wine or beer with a meal in a restaurant

You can buy fireworks
You can hold a licence to drive a moped, motor cycle, certain tractors or invalid carriages

At age 17
You can hold a licence to drive any vehicle except certain heavy ones
You can be sent to prison
You can appear before adult courts
You can engage in street trading

At age 18
You can leave home without your parents' consent
You can get married without your parents' consent
You can vote
You can act as executor of a person's will
You can make a will
You can see an '18' film
You can bet
You can change your name
You can apply for a passport
You can buy and sell goods
You can own houses and land
You can can buy on hire purchase
You can apply for a mortgage
You can sue and be sued
You can go abroad to sing, play or perform professionally
You can sit on a jury
You can be a blood donor
You can buy alcohol
You can drink alcohol in a pub

At age 21
You can stand in a parliamentary or local election
You can drive any mechanically propelled vehicle
You can hold a licence to sell alcohol
You can take part in a homosexual relationship (applies to boys only)
You can adopt a child

Source: *Rights, Responsibilities and the Law* Judith Edmunds, ILEA/Nelson, 1982, p. 13

There is an interesting relationship between adults and children in our society. Previous sources will have suggested that adults identify a large difference between themselves and children. This difference is especially important when adults want to spend their leisure time in each other's company. The next two sources throw some light on the place of children in adult leisure time.

ACTIVITY 4

(a) Looking at both the advert and the cartoon, make a list of assumptions about children and adults' views of children contained within them.
    Select words and phrases from source 2.8 which illustrate these ideas (eg 'menace').

(b) Source 2.9 is a comment not only on the relationship between adults and children, but also upon a mainly middle class move to change the style of the upbringing of children. What is this view, and what opinion does the cartoonist appear to have of it?

2.8

Are kids a menace to our pubs?

You may remember a couple of advertisements we ran late last year. (Then again, you may not.)

They dealt with the subject of our licensing laws on the one hand, and violence in pubs on the other.

They drew a very satisfying response. All together, 7,800 people sent in the forms or wrote letters.

More than a few of the respondents touched on the law as it relates to children in pubs.

So we thought we would raise the matter in an advertisement designed to test the strength of feeling that exists.

Dwell on the subject while making your way across a rain-swept pub car park carrying orangeades to the little ones, and it seems ridiculous that they can't sit inside where it's cosy and dry.

On the other hand, what about the other bloke's noisy little monsters. Do you really want them racketing around the bar when you've dropped in for a quiet pint and a chat?

Some people believe that allowing children into pubs will increase the chance of them becoming drunkards.

On the other hand, others feel that the presence of the family would curb any inclination Dad may have to blow his wages buying drinks for the boys.

So we would very much like to hear your views on the whole subject of children and pubs.

 WHITBREAD & CO LTD
Whitbread and Co.

2.9

"Nancy, if you insist on staying with the grownups—and of course we're delighted to have you—you must allow us to make an occasional remark that goes over your head."

B. Changes in Childhood

The view of childhood that has been identified in the last section is fairly new. It is also unique to Western industrialised societies. Evidence from the past suggests very different views of the role and perceived abilities of children, both in the family and in society as a whole.

ACTIVITY 5

Philippe Aries has studied the representation of childhood in Europe in the Middle Ages.

Read the extract from his book (2.11) and examine the detail from a 16th century painting by the artist Bruegel (2.10).

(a) Compare the different people in the picture. Is it possible to distinguish adults from children?
The painting is called 'Children's Games', so we must assume that some, at least, of the characters are children.

(b) How is the representation of children in the painting different from what we would expect today?

(c) How does Aries explain the image of children in painting like this?
Why, do you think, medieval society was 'younger' than today's?

2.10

Detail from 'Children's Games' by Bruegel, 1560 (Procession with Whitson bride)

2.11

Little adults

In medieval society the idea of childhood did not exist; this is not to suggest that children were neglected, forsaken or despised. The idea of childhood is not to be confused with affection for children: it corresponds to an awareness of the particular nature of childhood, that particular nature which distinguishes the child from the adult, even the young adult. In medieval society, this awareness was lacking. That is why, as soon as the child could live without the constant solicitude [care] of his mother, his nanny or his cradle-rocker, he belonged to adult society. That adult society now strikes us as rather puerile [childish]: no doubt this is largely a matter of its mental age, but it is also due to its physical age, because it was partly made up of children and youths.

Source: *Centuries of Childhood* by Philippe Aries, Penguin, Harmondsworth, 1973, p. 125

ACTIVITY 6

Historians of childhood have identified the beginnings of a formal education system as a major reason for the differences which people began to perceive between children and adults.

Read the extract from Aries (2.12)

(a) What effect does he see education as having on the status of children?

(b) Thinking about the education system that you have experienced, list the ways in which it could be said to
(i) separate children from adults.
(ii) prepare children for a new stage of life, 'adulthood'.

2.12

Medieval civilization ... knew nothing as yet of modern education. That is the main point: it had no idea of education. Nowadays our society depends, and knows that it depends, on the success of its educational system. It has a system of education, a concept of education, an awareness of its importance. New sciences such as psycho-analysis, pediatrics [a branch of medicine which specialises in children] and psychology devote themselves to the problems of childhood, and their findings are transmitted to parents by way of a mass of popular literature. Our world is obsessed by the physical, moral and sexual problems of childhood.

This preoccupation was unknown to medieval civilization, because there was no problem for the Middle Ages: as soon as he had been weaned, or soon after, the child became the natural companion of the adult.

Source: Aries, *op. cit.* p. 395

ACTIVITY 7

With the idea of childhood as a time of education for adult life came many changes in the way of life of upper class children.

Paintings began to show great differences between children and adults.

(a) Describe the child in the painting by Millais. ('The Nest' mid-19th century)

(b) Compare the child with the adult, noting particularly the clothes, facial expressions and apparent focus of interest of each.

(c) Now compare this painting with source 2.11. Draw up a table to summarise the differences between adults and children in the two periods of history, as shown by paintings.

2.13

The Victorian upper classes separated their children from adult society almost entirely and had clear ideas about the place of children.

ACTIVITY 8

Read the three extracts which describe life for the Victorian child, and look at the picture.

(a) Note down the ideas they suggest about childhood in the 19th century, under the following headings:
   – relationships with parents
   – children's 'needs'
   – discipline
   – values to be learned.

(b) Look back at section A of this unit and write a short statement about childhood today under each of the same headings.

2.14

I can never remember being bathed by my mother, or even having my hair brushed by her, and I should not at all have liked it if she had done anything of the kind. We did not feel it was her place to do such things; though my father used to cut our finger-nails with his sharp white-handled knife, and that felt quite pleasant and proper. Anyhow, there was no need for my mother to do such things, for Nana hardly ever went out, and if she did the housemaid or the nurserymaid was left in charge of us. (*Period Piece*, published in 1960)

Source: *Finding out about Victorian Childhood*, Batsford, London, 1986, p. 9

2.15

In the windows of the day nursery there should be boxes of flowers...to teach the little ones of the country, and of the nursery rhymes and fairy tales they love so well. Let the walls be papered with some pleasant paper, in which the colours shall be bright and cheerful...A band of colour might be made by buying some of the Christmas books, which Mr. H.S. Marks, R.A., Miss Kate Greenaway, and Mr. Walter Crane have so charmingly and artistically illustrated, and by pasting the scenes in regular order and procession, as a kind of frieze under the upper band of distemper [paint], varnished over to protect from dirt.

Decoration and Furniture of Town Houses (1881)

Source: *Finding out about Victorian Childhood*, Batsford, London, 1986, p. 9

2.17

Have you not heard, what dreadful plagues,
Are threatened by the Lord,
To him who breaks his father's laws,
Or mocks his mother's word?

What heavy guilt upon him lies!
How cursed is his name!
The ravens shall pick out his eyes
And eagles eat the same.

Source: *Divine Song* by Isaac Watts, OUP, Oxford, 1971

2.16

Rich Victorian children are paraded by their nanny to meet visiting adults

During the Industrial Revolution in Britain, many of the workers in the factories, mines and mills were children.
The way of life of the working class child was sharply contrasted to that of the middle and upper class child.

ACTIVITY 9

Compare the two photographs of children taken at the turn of the century.

What do they tell you about different views of upper class and working class childhood?

2.18

2.19

ACTIVITY 10

Child labour was much criticised throughout the 19th century by middle class philanthropists.

Robert Southey was one such critic.
Read the account of a conversation between himself and a manufacturer, written by Southey.

(a)   List the arguments given by the manufacturer to justify child labour.

(b)   What reasons does Southey give for the existence of child labour?

(c)   What is Southey's view and how do we know that he held this view?

2.20

A conversation between Southey and a Manchester gentleman who is showing him over the cotton factories.

Mr._____ remarked that nothing could be so beneficial to a country as manufacture. 'You see these children, sir,' said he. 'In most parts of England poor children are a burthen to their parents and to the parish; here the parish, which would else have to support them, is rid of all expense; they get their bread almost as soon as they can run about, and by the time they are seven or eight years old bring in the money. There is no idleness among us: they come at five in the morning; we allow them half an hour for breakfast, and an hour for dinner; they leave work at six, and another set relieves them for the night; the wheels never stand still.' I was looking, while he spoke, at the unnatural dexterity with which the fingers of these little creatures were playing in the machinery, half giddy myself with the noise and the endless motion.

'These children,' I said, 'have no time to receive instruction.' 'That, sir,' he replied 'is the evil which we have found. Girls are employed here from the age you see them till they marry, and then they know nothing about domestic work, not even how to mend a stocking or boil a potato. But we are remedying this now, and send the children to school for an hour after they have done work.'

It would have been in vain to argue had I been disposed to it. Mr._____ was a man of humane and kindly nature, who would not himself use anything cruelly, and judged of others by his own feelings. I thought of the cities in Arabian romance, where all the inhabitants were enchanted: here Commerce is the Queen witch, and I had no talisman strong enough to disenchant those who were daily drinking of the golden cup of her charms.

Source: *Letters from England* 1807 by Robert Southey

Part of the argument for factory reform was related to the demands that state education be provided for all children.

Although many people advocated education for all, the reasons greatly varied, and therefore the *type* of education demanded varied.

ACTIVITY 11

(a)   Looking again at source 2.20, decide what the manufacturer sees as the purpose of education.

(b)   Read extracts 2.21, 2.22 and 2.23

In each case decide for what purpose education for the working class is being supported.

(c)   Which groups in society do you think would have held each view?

2.21

The preservation of internal peace, not less than the improvement of our national institutions, depends on the education of the working classes . . .

[The poor must] be made to understand their political position in society and the duties that belong to it . . . that they are infinitely more interested in the preservation of public tranquility than any other class of society; that mechanical inventions and discoveries are always supremely advantageous to them; and that their real interests can only be effectually promoted by their displaying greater prudence and forethought.

Source: J. Kay 'The Moral and Physical Condition of the Working Class in Manchester in 1832' quoted in *History of Education 1780–1870* Brian Simon, Lawrence and Wishart, London, 1960, p. 168

2.22

Think you a corrupt Government could perpetuate its exclusive and demoralising influence amid a people . . . united and instructed? Could a vicious aristocracy find its servile slaves to render homage to idleness and idolatry to the wealth too often fraudulently exacted from industry? . . . Could corruption sit in the judgement seat . . . if the millions were educated in a knowledge of their rights? No, no, friends; and hence the efforts of the exclusive few to keep the people ignorant and divided.

Source: 'Address on Education' London Working Men's Association 1837 quoted in Simon *op. cit*. p. 223

2.23

My plan of instruction is extremely simple and limited. They learn, on weekdays, such coarse works as may fit them for servants. I allow of no writing for the poor. My object is not to make then fanatics, but to train up the lower classes in habits of industry and piety.

Source: Hannah More, 1790 (head of a Sunday School) 'The Letters of Hannah More' R. Brimley Johnson (ed) 1925 p. 183 quoted in Simon *op. cit*.

C. Childhood and social class

The legislation controlling child labour, together with the introduction of compulsory state education, produced some changes in the status of working class children during the early part of the 20th century. However, many families were poor and still needed their children's income.

ACTIVITY 12

The two extracts refer to child labour in Britain nearly 80 years apart.

Compare the evidence from the two sources and answer the following questions.

(a) What legislation exists in each case to protect children?

(b) How easy is the legislation to flout?

(c) What does the tone of the newspaper article suggest about the journalist's own opinion of her findings?

2.24

An Edwardian childhood

Thirteen I left school and I went and got a job as a van boy. But I left school when I was about twelve really 'cause I don't suppose I done three months' schooling in the year. Always out after money, you know, pocket money really. 'Cause as I say I always worked the trick – either I was bad with me leg or else, I got ringworms or something, always worked it like that. That's why the school board was so hot on me. If I hadn't been crippled you know where I'd have gone – truant school. Most of the boys they used to work at the railways, van boys. Well one of them said to me 'Ere – over the railways yard', he said, 'The yard shed,' he said ... 'Compton wants a van boy, why don't you go after it?'
I'd say, 'No, I'm not fourteen yet.'
'Don't matter, tell him you're fourteen.'
'Course they didn't ask for birth certificates, we had no insurance cards or anything like that then. I went over, I said, 'You want a van boy sir?'
'How old are you?'
'Fourteen sir.'
'Oh, when can you start?'
'Now sir' (four o'clock in the afternoon). 'Now sir', you know, so eager to get the job.
'All right – start in the morning.'
'Right'. Well we used to work Borough Market, Billingsgate Market and all round. 'Course it was hours and hours – eighteen hours a day sometimes. All for five shillings a week. But my mother was fair. She used to give me half a crown out of the five shilling.
'Course the other half crown went in beer.

Source: Thomas Morgan, born London, 1892, in *Edwardian Childhoods* by Thea Thompson, RKP, London, 1981, p. 29

2.25

School holidays scandal of a million child workers
by EILEEN MacDONALD

MORE THAN a million under-age schoolchildren in Britain are working illegally during summer holidays—many for as little as 2p an hour. Others are physically at risk.

The Observer visited a number of clothing manufacturers and back-street factories in north London. Out of six, we found that two were willing to employ under-age children.

We visited Mr Kostas of Unit C, Spencer Avenue, Wood Green, asking for work for a 12-year-old boy, a nephew. Mr Kostas, an out-worker for dress manufacturers, Miss Sam Ltd, said he would offer him £15 for working a 45-hour week.

The job, explained the factory owner, would be to pick pieces of cotton off the floor, carry loads of dresses, and tidy up.

Mr Kostas said he would not be the only 12-year-old working for him. 'There are lots of them that age we use. He would have com-pany.' The boy could work from 9 a.m. to 6 p.m. during his school holiday, and then 'we could fit him in' when term restarted.

When we confronted Mr Kostas, he refused to comment on illegally employing children. A spokesman for Miss Sam Ltd said: 'It is noth-ing to do with us. It is his own fac-tory. We don't know anything about it.'

In Tottenham, a carpet manufac-turer was willing to employ a 14-year-old boy. His job would be to stand on a stool above a running loom and ensure that the shuttles were working correctly. The firm refused to be drawn on

pay, saying they would have to see the boy first.

The Health and Safety Executive reckoned this would be a danger-ous job, and are currently investi-gating this case and Mr Kostas's claim to employing under-age workers.

Under the present law:
■ Children under 13 cannot work in a part-time job.
■ It is illegal for anyone under 18 to work any machine in motion.
■ A child under 16 cannot work in a factory unless other members of his or her family work there.
■ Children under 15 cannot work on a Saturday or any other school holiday for more than four hours.

The Anti-Slavery Society is pro-ducing a report on a survey of 449 children aged between six and 16. Many worked in shops,

supermarkets and factories and some appeared to be physically at risk in the jobs they were expected to do.

A spokesman said: 'The law governing child employment is a mess. Employers know it and often children are being exploited. During school holidays it gets worse because employers lower the age limit, and in many cases the wages as well.'

The Low Pay Unit, which has questioned 1,700 schoolchildren, found 26 per cent of London chil-dren were working under-age, out of a total of 83 per cent working illegally. Most were working for less than £1 an hour and 10 per cent for less than 50p. One boy was given the equivalent of 2p an hour for helping his mother clean offices.

Source: *The Observer*, 30.8.87.

Between 1977 and 1980, a group of doctors and academics studied health in Britain. The resulting report, *Inequalities in Health* was summarised by Anna Coote in a *New Statesman* article. She claimed that the report had been 'hushed-up'. The report suggested that a person's health is largely influenced by his/her social class, especially in the early years of life.

ACTIVITY 13

(a) What does the bar chart (2.26) show about the mortality rate of children in Social Classes I to V?

(b) Using source 2.27 suggest reasons for the figures in the bar chart.

(c) List all the aspects of life which might influence the health of a child, and suggest what part social class inequality might play in each.

2.26

Social class and child mortality

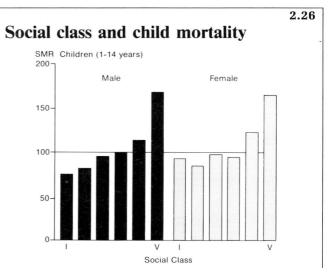

SMR = Standardised Mortality Ratio. It is a measure of the deviation of mortality rate from the average which is shown on the table as 100.

Source: *Occupational Mortality: 1970–72* (HMSO, London, 1978)

2.27

Health and social class

Although working class children are more vulnerable to fatal injury and illness . . . their parents are less likely than those in the middle classes to take them to the doctor. This may have more to do with the quality of care and the costs (financial and otherwise) which the parents anticipate, than with any unreasonable response to sickness. For it is well-known that health services in predominantly working class areas are less accessible and of a poorer quality . . .

People with lower incomes eat, and feed their children, more harmful foods; they smoke more and take less exercise. These habits are not simply a product of working class culture, but reflect a relative lack of 'material security and advantage'. Resources which improve the quality of parental care tend to be material – such as 'sufficient household income, a safe, uncrowded and unpolluted home, warmth and hygiene, a means of rapid communication with the outside world, eg telephone or car, and an adequate level of man or woman power.

Source: Anna Coote 'Death to the Working Class' in *New Statesman*, 12 September 1980, pp. 8–9

D.   Childhood and gender

Throughout history, and still today, the sex of a child has largely influenced his/her treatment, life chances and hence self-perceptions.

ACTIVITY 14

Read extracts 2.28 and 2.29 which relate to the advice given 19th century mothers about the care of their children.

(a) Decide how the Victorians explained the differences between the behaviour of girls and boys.

Many government inquiries were conducted into child labour in the last century. The *Parliamentary Papers* of 1842, quoted from in source 2.28, give evidence of the way of life of some working class girls.

This extract, in particular, illustrates social attitudes towards girls held by the authors of the *Papers*.

(b) Read the extract and decide what these attitudes are.

(c) Compare the evidence in sources 2.28 and 2.29. What differences and similarities are shown in attitudes towards middle/upper class girls and working class girls?

2.28

'A very ignorant child'

Susan Pitchforth, aged 11, living at Elland: I have worked at this pit going two years. Come to work at eight or before, but I set off from home at seven. I walk a mile and a half to my work, both in winter and summer. I get porridge for breakfast before I come, and bring my dinner with me—a muffin. When I have done about twelve loads I eat it while at work. I run 24 corves a day; I cannot come up till I have done them all. If I want to relieve myself I go into any part of the pit. Sometimes the boys see me when they go by. My father slaps me sometimes upon the head, or upon the back, so as to make me cry. . .

A very ignorant child (commented Mr Scriven, the Sub-Commissioner). She stood shivering before me from cold. The rag that hung about her waist was once called a shift, which is as black as the coal she thrusts, and saturated with water, from the dripping of the roof and shaft. During my examination of her the banksman whom I had left in the pit came to the public-house and wanted to take her away, because, as he expressed himself, it was not *decent* that she should be (her person) *exposed* to us; oh no! it was criminal above ground; and, like the two or three other colliers in the cabin, he became evidently mortified that these deeds of darkness should be brought to light.

Source: *Parliamentary Papers* 1842, vol. XVII, p. 104

Childhood and gender

2.29

Walking and other out-of-door exercises cannot be too much recommended to young people. Even skating, driving hoop and other boyish sports may be practised to great advantage by little girls provided they can be pursued within the enclosure of a garden or court; in the street, of course, they would be highly improper. It is true, such games are rather violent, and sometimes noisy, but they tend to form a vigorous constitution; and girls who are habitually lady-like, will never allow themselves to be rude and vulgar, even in play.

Source: *The Little Girl's Own Book* Lydia Maria Child, Robert Martin, 1847

In play, as in learning, Victorian mothers were advised that within the family, the two sexes should as small children share many activities. Shared play, it was believed, would encourage both suitable similarities, and at the same time, reinforce and develop those sex differences that were assumed to be 'natural'. The general assumption was made that boys were naturally assertive, and girls were naturally gentle and passive. By playing together, each sex would develop some of the traits of the opposite sex – 'the girl's weakness [would be] strengthened, and the boy's roughness softened' – but as well, each would bring out appropriate behaviour in the other. For a boy, it was suggested that contact with his sisters would develop 'an instinct of protectiveness which it is well to encourage, since it is the germ of true manly feelings in after life.'

Source: *The Victorian Girl and the Feminine Ideal* Deborah Gorham, Croom Helm, 1982, p. 75

Education for young women was becoming more common for the middle classes, but there were efforts by some to discourage it.

Appropriate education, especially for working class girls, was seen as being training in domesticity.

ACTIVITY 15

(a) Look at sources 2.30 and 2.31

What conclusions do they help you draw about education for girls, working class and middle class, in the last century?

(b) Consider the extent to which there have been changes in this situation, using the statistics from the Inner London Education Authority (2.32).

2.30

Nursery Rhymes for the Times

Sally was a pretty girl
Fanny was her sister;
Sally read all night and day
Fanny sighed and kissed her.

Sally won some school degrees
Fanny won a lover;
Sally soundly rated her,
And thought herself above her.

Fanny had a happy home,
And urged that plea only;
Sally she was learned – and
Also she was lonely.

Source: *Punch*, 20.2.1875

2.31

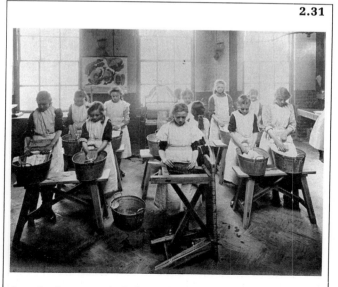

Learning how to wash clothes, Clapham, 1900

2.32

Examination entries, ILEA, 1983

A-level (1983)	Girls	Boys
Maths	30%	70%
Physics	26%	74%
Chemistry	38%	62%

	CSE		O-Level		A-Level	
	Girls	Boys	Girls	Boys	Girls	Boys
Biology	70%	30%	62%	38%	64%	36%
English	51%	49%	55%	45%	76%	25%
French	67%	33%	62%	38%	80%	20%
Home Economics	91%	9%	90%	10%	100%	nil

Differences between the upbringing of girls and boys is still very common today.
It is not only schools which can be seen as differentiating between boys and girls. There are many examples in the mass media (television, comics, advertisements, stories etc.).

ACTIVITY 16
Extracts 2.33 and 2.34 are taken from a toy catalogue and a comic.

(a) Decide what they suggest about the different
  (i) supposed interests
  (ii) assumed future roles
of boys and girls.

(b) List other ways that similar sex-role socialisation occurs in our society.

2.33

Source: *Woolworths Christmas Catalogue*, 1986

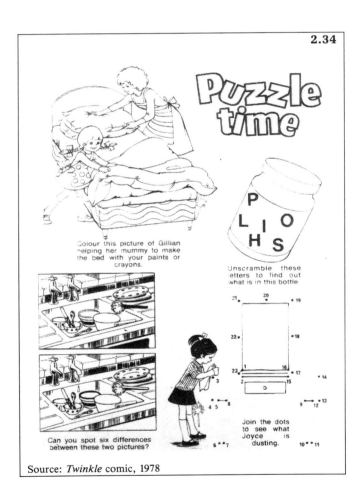

2.34

Colour this picture of Gillian helping her mummy to make the bed with your paints or crayons.

Unscramble these letters to find out what is in this bottle

Can you spot six differences between these two pictures?

Join the dots to see what Joyce is dusting.

Source: *Twinkle* comic, 1978

E.   Conclusion

As we saw in Section A, childhood is often regarded as a time of innocence and contentment, and the nuclear family is seen as a haven for children.

However, in spite of this commonly held view, abuse of children within the family does occur. Child abuse is frequently in the news. It might even be currently described as a 'moral panic'.

ACTIVITY 17

Read again the figures quoted in the *Guardian* article at the beginning of this chapter (source 2.3)

(a) Consider what problems there might be in collecting figures on child abuse.

(b) Source 2.35 suggests that child abuse is not new. From the evidence in this chapter can you suggest reasons for current concern about the subject.

Sources 2.36 and 2.37 look at the rights of a parent over a child, and the rights of a child.

(c) What conflicts between the rights of parents and of children are suggested by these two sources?

2.35

When I was a child, some fifty to sixty years ago, childhood was looked upon as the most harmonious part of life. Parental love was always close to perfection. Child abuse was not recognized, not even by the medical profession, in spite of the fact that hundreds of children in practically all countries, including the most developed ones, were killed or incapacitated for life by physical abuse every year. . . We know today beyond doubt that children are often abused, physically as well as mentally, and that children are often neglected. We also know that there are parents who are indifferent, or even actively hostile to their children.

Source: 'Child Victims of Armed Conflict' opening remarks to NGO report by Professor Holger Lundback, April 1984

2.36

The 'Rights of the Child' is a problematic idea in itself since the term 'right' implies a relationship between two people, one asserting a claim and the other recognizing or guaranteeing it. In the case of children the 'claim' is usually against parents, and evokes strong reactions:

'. . .observe the number of adults/parents who feel genuinely threatened by the mention of children's rights, as if there were a finite quantity to "rights" in each family and giving some to children would mean taking some from parents.' (Smyke, 1978).

It is, perhaps, hard to concede children's rights when it appears that by doing so parental or family interests are undermined. In the context of a loving and stable family, children may have no real need of rights. But surely in cases of child abuse and neglect, it is clear that children must have a right not only to protection, but also to proper independent representation in legal proceedings, and the right to express their views, even though these will inevitably infringe parental autonomy and family privacy.

Source: *Children* MRG Report No. 69, Jo Boyden and Andy Hudson

---

2.37

Under the banner of children's rights, the state has gradually eroded the power of parents over their children. In certain circumstances the local authority can take a child 'into care', even against the wishes of the parents. There are currently over 100,000 children in care. Current opinion tends to be unenthusiastic about institutionalized care. Since the 1960s the view that the needy child's natural family should be supported as far as possible to enable it to keep the child has also waned in popularity. Fostering is now more widely favoured, a policy which seems to put the principle of practical care above that of natural family relationships. The trend towards substitute care increased following the 1975 Children's Act.

Source: *Age and Generation* Mike O'Donnell, Tavistock, London, 1985, p. 20

As we have seen, during the twentieth century childhood has become a stage of a person's life quite separate and different from all the rest. It has also become a longer period of time, as young people are controlled by an increasing number of laws and have to stay on at school longer.

Children have been studied and described and their 'needs' have been identified by a growing number of 'experts' like paediatricians, teachers, child psychologists and youth workers. A whole new area of enterprise surrounds toys, books, games, clothes and holidays aimed specifically at children.

And yet, at the same time, young people suffer from confused expectations of what adults want from them; and the expectation is different for different groups of children. At times children are protected and at others they are exploited. As young people reach adolescence, their so-called 'problems' could be related to the confused role they have in our industrialised society.

The interesting question for the sociologist is how the age-stage of childhood has been socially constructed and how this construction will develop.

Further reading

Aires, P. *Centuries of Childhood*, Penguin, Harmondsworth, 1973
Beecham, Y., Fiehn, J., Gates, J. *Childhood: A Study in Socialisation*, Harrap/Nelson, London, 1980
Boyden, J., Hudson, A. *Children* Minority Rights Group, Report No. 69
Thompson, T. *Edwardian Childhoods*, RKP, London, 1981
TUC *All Work and No Play*, 1985

UNIT 3   The Working Class

> 'The proletarians have nothing to lose but their chains. They have a world to win.'
> Marx and Engels *The Communist Manifesto*, 1848
>
> '. . . it has become doubtful whether speaking of the working class still makes much sense.' Ralf Dahrendorf *Class and Class Conflict in Industrial Society*, 1959

These quotes highlight two very different views of the working class. The aim of this unit is to look at the arguments and evidence which give rise to such polarised views.

Before you start to look at the sociological account of the working class use the following exercise (Activity 1) to dig out your own stereotype of the typical working class character.

ACTIVITY 1
Construct a stereotype of a 20 year old working class male and female. Do this by listing the most typical examples of the following; name, dress, mode of transport, hobbies, politics, favourite paper, drink, music, food and holiday, way of saying 'hello' and 'good-bye'.

Sally and Kevin – a view of a young working class couple from 'Coronation Street'.

Sociologists are divided over whether we really can talk of 'the working class' as if this group had some sort of separate identity and shared experience. Some feel it was useful to analyse society in strictly class terms but that changing social conditions now make this redundant. The sections which follow contain some of the evidence produced by sociologists to support their particular view of the working class. But before this issue can be dealt with it is important to decide exactly what the term 'class' means.

A.   The Nature of Class

ACTIVITY 2
Using extracts 3.1–3.3 and source 3.4 produce a summary definition of class in under 30 words.

3.1

Insofar as millions of families under economic conditions of existence that separate their mode of life, their interests and their culture from those of the other classes, and put them in hostile opposition to the latter, they form a class.

Source: Karl Marx *The Eighteenth Brumaire of Louis Bonaparte* 1852

3.2

A social class can perhaps be rather cumbersomely described as a group of people with certain common traits: descent, education, accent, similarity of occupation, wealth, moral attitudes, friends, hobbies, accommodation; and with generally similar ideas, and forms of behaviour, who meet each other on equal terms, and regard themselves as belonging to one group.

Source: Jilly Cooper *Class* (Corgi, London, 1980)

3.3

(the idea of class always) entails the notion of historical relationship . . . the relationship must always be embodied in real people and in a real context . . . class happens when some men, as a result of common experiences (inherited or shared), feel and articulate the identity of their interests as between themselves, and as against other men whose interests are different from (and usually opposed to) theirs.

Source: E.P. Thompson *The Making of the English Working Class* (Penguin, Harmondsworth, 1974)

3.4

Walking to Ascot – a view from the other side of the fence

B. The Old Working Class

The old or 'traditional' working class has given rise to a mixture of nostalgic and critical writing. Richard Hoggart and Jeremy Seabrook are both well known for describing their working class upbringings (the former in the 1920s and 30s, the latter in the 1940s). Willmott and Young's classic study of family and community was researched a little later between 1953 and 1955.

ACTIVITY 3

(a) Using sources 3.5–3.8, list the main features of the working class community.

(b) What do think would be the advantages and disadvantages of living in such a community?

3.5

In Bethnal Green the person who says he 'knows everyone' is, of course, exaggerating, but pardonably so. He does, with various degrees of intimacy, know many people outside (but often through) his family, and it is this which makes it, in the view of many informants, a 'friendly place'. Bethnal Green, or at any rate the precinct, is, it appears, a community which has some sense of being one. There is a sense of community, that is a feeling of solidarity between people who occupy the common territory, which springs from the fact that people and their families have lived there a long time.

Source: Michael Young and Peter Willmott *Family and Kinship in East London* (Penguin, Harmondsworth, 1962)

3.6

As a kid, they were very narrow minded where we lived. One woman in our street, she used to have a bloke round while her husband was working. The women of the street all got together, and they came round to my mother's house to decide what they should do about this woman's carrying on. They had a proper council of war. It was like a bloody parliament, our front room. In the end, they elected a deputation to go round and talk to this woman. They told her she had to give it up, and then they'd be magnanimous and not tell her husband.

Source: Jeremy Seabrook *Working-class Childhood* (Gollanz, London, 1982)

3.7

Home may be private, but the front door opens out of the living-room on to the street, and when you go down the one step or use it as a seat on a warm evening you become part of the life of the neighbourhood. To a visitor they are understandably depressing, these massed proletarian areas; street after regular street of shoddily uniform houses intersected by a dark pattern of ginnels and snickets (alley-ways) and courts; mean, squalid and in a permanent half-fog... But to the insider, these are small worlds, each as homogeneous (uniform) and well-defined as a village. Down below, on the main road running straight into town, the bosses' cars whirr away at five o'clock to converted farm-houses ten miles out in the hills; the men stream up into their district. They know it, as do all its inhabitants, in intimate detail – automatically slipping up a snicket here or through a shared lavatory block there; they know it as a group of tribal areas.

Source: Richard Hoggart *The Uses of Literacy* (Penguin, Harmondsworth, 1958)

3.8

Closing time – Sunday afternoon

But the reality of life for many working people was extremely harsh. There may well have been, and may still be, something warm and supportive about life in an established community, but the other side of the coin was often a life of extreme deprivation and suffering. Extract 3.9 is a personal account by a male mill hand in Bolton in 1937 of his job. Extract 3.10 is a description of claiming 'Assistance' by Daisy Noakes, again from the 1930s.

ACTIVITY 4
Using your own knowledge and understanding and sources 3.5–3.10 write down those aspects of working class life you think have changed over the last 50 years or so, and what may still be similar.

3.9

The fact that I had a cold, that the atmosphere was particularly vile, and that the day was dull, were first impressions, which gave rise to feelings of the rottenness of the system under which we live. The general feeling in the spinning room (worst paid workers) is that work is an evil thing, a thing to be got over as quickly as possible. I thought of the servility of the English people in standing the bad system of working, $8\frac{3}{4}$ hours a day in a putrid atmosphere for meagre wages and always feeling below par.

I got the impression that the atmosphere, the electric lights burning (all bad lights), everything combined had an effect on the temper of everyone, spinners, piecers, bobbin carriers, etc. The feeling of futility was a constant one during this day (more so than usual), to see the people wasting their lives (mine in particular) at such an occupation. To know that every piecer dislikes the life he leads at work, and to see how conditioned he has to become, he curses rails and dreams, but he comes up every day for more. For more bad air. For more slow painful hours. For meagre wages.

Source: Humphrey Jennings and Charles Madge (Editors) *Mass-Observation Day-Survey May 12 1937* (Faber and Faber, London, 1987)

ACTIVITY 5
Both the mill hand (3.9) and Daisy Noakes (3.10) are badly treated by people in authority over them. Why do you think they put up with this treatment?

3.10

I went down on Sunday morning, gave my name at a reception desk and was told to go through a curtain door and wait. Behind that door was a passage with forms on either side on which people were sitting who looked a lot worse off than me, rag and bone men, down-and-outs, but we were all here for the same purpose. Money for survival. A peaked cap gentleman walked up and down kicking a foot here and there, and should anyone try to make conversation shouted 'Quiet please no talking'. We all sat like dummies. Every so often, a name was called, and the person went into a room, then back to resume his seat. Mine was called. I went through the door, but no further into the room. I stood as requested, with my back to the door, while about ten men sitting round a table asked me questions. All they wanted to know was, what I had been living on till then, and had I any more savings anywhere. I then went back to my place on the form. This continued until new applicants had been seen, then an opening like a ticket office at a railway station removed its shutter, and the pay out began. The man inside shouted a name then the peaked cap gentleman shouted it. The money was slammed down as it was counted, so everybody knew what everybody else was getting. 'Hurry along' was heard all the time, as if they were glad to be rid of the dregs of the community.

Source: Daisy Noakes *Faded Rainbow* (Queen Sparks Books, Brighton, 1980)

C.   The Affluent Worker

Class divisions are not as clear-cut today as they were in the 1930s. Post-war increases in the standard of living and the development of the welfare state together with slum clearance and increased movement around the country seemed to have put an end to a working class way of life in traditional communities. It also led to the infamous 'Embourgeoisement Thesis', meaning that the working class was becoming just like everybody else, 'bourgeois' or middle class.

The 'Affluent Worker' study by John Goldthorpe and his colleagues looked at the impact of affluence on working class life. Researched in the 1960s the study used Luton as a prosperous example of post-war British society with a relatively mobile population.

Writing in the 1980s, the political scientist, Ivor Crewe and the sociologist, Steven Lukes make claims which echo the Affluent Worker findings. Ideas of 'split' 'division' or 'sections' within the working class crop up frequently.

Of course, we must be very cautious here. Crewe and the Affluent Worker team were writing two decades apart about rather different splits within the class system. The authors of the Luton study were very cautious in suggesting a division between affluent and traditional workers, but the evidence seems to point towards there being new divisions in the working class, and these seem to be well illustrated by patterns of housing tenure, shown in extract 3.14

ACTIVITY 6

(a)   Using extracts 3.11–3.13 list the characteristics of the 'new', more affluent, working class.

(b)   Outline the possible consequences of a divided working class eg in terms of voting behaviour, class solidarity etc.

3.11

The Affluent Worker study

What changes, then, if any have occurred in the life of the relatively affluent worker? The most important has been the 'privatisation' of the worker and his family with home centredness consequently amplified; the manual worker's family and its fortunes become his 'central life interest'.

Secondly, although unionism is still strong, it expresses an instrumental rather than solidaristic orientation: that is, the newly affluent worker is likely to regard the union as the means to a particular end: e.g. he no longer sees union membership as the expression of a strong, ideological, working class solidarity . . . privatisation and instrumentalism, encourage 'a more individualistic outlook' among the manual workers, with a simultaneous weakening of communal and kin orientations.

Source: Bilton, T. *et al. Introductory Sociology* (Macmillan, Basingstoke, 1987)

3.12

Class and the 1983 Election

Manual workers can therefore be divided into the 'traditional and the 'new' working class. In 1983 these two groups voted very differently . . . Among the traditional working class of trade unionists and council house tenants, and in the traditional strongholds of Scotland and the North, Labour remains the first, if not always the majority, choice. But among the new working class of manual workers who live in the South, who own their own home and who do not belong to a trade union, the Conservatives have established a clear lead over Labour. Indeed, Labour trails in third place, behind the Alliance, in the first two categories. It is as if the two groups of manual workers belong to quite different social classes.

Source: Ivor Crewe 'Can Labour rise again?' *Social Studies Review* Vol. 1 No. 1 1985

3.13

A divided working class?

More and more, the working class is concerned with issues of consumption – of housing and of state benefits, for example. According to Lukes, recent research shows Britain to be a society divided against itself in new ways: those with a stake in private property and those without; the self sufficient on wages versus welfare claimants; the populations of declining regions against those resident in economically buoyant areas; those in relatively secure occupational or company career ladders against the unemployed and subemployed who are on the economic margins of society.

Source: Gordon Marshall, 'What is Happening to the Working Class?' *Social Studies Review* Vol. 2. No. 3.

ACTIVITY 7
If you were a political speech writer which statistics would you choose to show:
(i) The old class divisions are disappearing.
(ii) The working class and middle class remain divided.

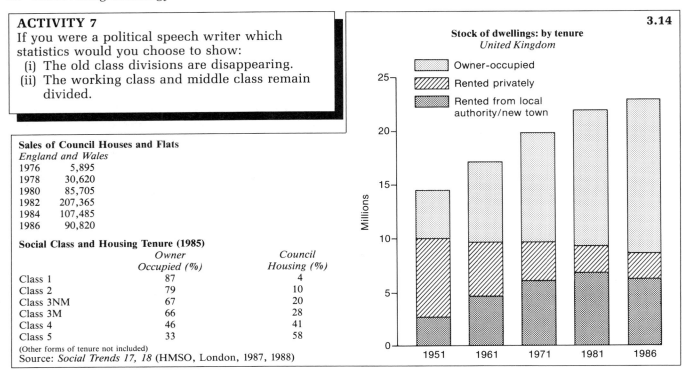

3.14

Stock of dwellings: by tenure
United Kingdom

Owner-occupied
Rented privately
Rented from local authority/new town

Sales of Council Houses and Flats
England and Wales

1976	5,895
1978	30,620
1980	85,705
1982	207,365
1984	107,485
1986	90,820

Social Class and Housing Tenure (1985)

	Owner Occupied (%)	Council Housing (%)
Class 1	87	4
Class 2	79	10
Class 3NM	67	20
Class 3M	66	28
Class 4	46	41
Class 5	33	58

(Other forms of tenure not included)
Source: *Social Trends 17, 18* (HMSO, London, 1987, 1988)

D.   A Fragmented Class

If, for the sake of argument, we accept some sort of internal division within the working class between newer and older forms of consumption patterns, attitudes and behaviour, then we could go on to ask the question – are there any other distinct or different groups within the working class? Are there any other sections of the working class with different interests and experiences? If so, is it reasonable to talk about a *fragmented* working class?

Ken Pryce's study of a West Indian ghetto in Bristol (3.15) is the complete opposite of the earlier romantic descriptions of the working class. In particular he emphasises a lack of community and social cohesion. Joanna Mack's evidence (3.16) is a chilling reminder of the extent of real poverty, of the growing numbers of people some believe are forming an 'underclass' at the base of society. Jeremy Seabrook (3.17) depicts workers in the service sector, each group encapsulated in its own little world.

All three extracts illustrate the diversity of modern working class experience and how it has, and in some ways has not, changed in the last 50 years.
This diversity is acknowledged even by the Marxist historian, Eric Hobsbawn. He sees 'a growing division of workers into sections and groups, each pursuing its own economic interest irrespective of the rest'.

ACTIVITY 8
Superficially, the evidence (3.15–3.17) could be read as indicating a total break-up of the working class. But is is open to more than one interpretation.

Referring back to the definitions of class (extracts 3.1–3.3), how could the evidence be interpreted:

(i) to show the existence of a fragmented working class

(ii) to show that there is something these different groups do share and therefore to recognise an identifiable working class?

3.15
● approximately 3 million people in Britain today cannot afford to heat the living areas of their homes
● around 6 million go without some essential aspect of clothing – such as a warm waterproof coat – because of lack of money
● nearly 3.5 million people do not have consumer durables such as carpets, a washing machine or a fridge because of lack of money
● at least 5.5 million people cannot afford basic items of food such as meat or fish every other day, a roast joint once a week or two hot meals a day

Source: Joanna Mack & Stewart Lansley *Poor Britain* (Allen & Unwin, London, 1985)

3.16

Today St. Paul's is essentially a residual neighbourhood suffering from rapidly deteriorating 'blight conditions'. The term 'Shanty Town' expresses not only the broken down state of the physical framework of St. Paul's; it refers as well to the transience and the lack of social cohesion and community in the area. It is the free-for-all openness of the place and this element of instability, combined with the squalor and the perils of decay which are responsible for the conception of St. Paul's as a shanty town... The dilapidation of St. Paul's is reflected in its shops. The local government councillor for the area is on record as saying that 'some of the existing shops are like a tin of worms – full of movement. They continually change hands'. St. Paul's, he noted, abounds with second-hand clothing shops...

The lack of community in St. Paul's is often not apparent to the stranger visiting the area for the first time, especially students and intellectuals with their tendency to romanticise the deviant and the exotic. Diverse groups with vastly dissimilar backgrounds do mingle freely in close physical interaction in St. Paul's. But this is deceptive, for mingling of this kind does not automatically create a community spirit in the sense of conformity, consensus and vigilance about community standards. The only unity is an external one, in the form of common services used by all. Beneath the romantic's illusion of a tight-knit, friendly, organic, warm, harmonious community, the divisions are deep.

Source: Ken Pryce *Endless Pressure* (Penguin, Harmondsworth, 1979)

St. Paul's, Bristol

3.17

We are barely aware of those [workers]...enclosed in offices that are smooth cliffs of granite and glass, with chipboard partitions pinned with holiday postcards, gunmetal cabinets and vending machines and a man-made climate that dries the nose and makes the throat permanently sore; those locked onto word processors and visual display units with the shimmering green figures, that leave such a persistent after-image on the retina and blur the black print of the evening paper; the shadowless glare of white strip-lighting, the finger-prints in the dust on the slats of the blind, the Busy Lizzie in the cottage cheese container, the lunch of dry Ryvita and golden delicious apples...

There is a whole population who are in the service of merchandise – not just selling, but in distribution, those heavy lorryloads that crowd the motorways, the watchful look and the dancing mascot in the cab, the cigarettes and the pop music and the Page Three girl and pint mugs at the service station...

Jeremy Seabrook *Landscapes of Poverty* (Blackwell, Oxford, 1985)

E. Working Class Women

Another fundamental change in the working class is in the role of women. Extracts 3.18 and 3.19 describe traditional working class attitudes. Paul Willis offers us the views of the adolescent male. The girl's role is seen as domestic and inferior. Valerie Hey's book on pubs uses evidence from research in Herefordshire and Mass Observation material to paint a familiar picture of sexism in the pub.

ACTIVITY 9

(a) Why might male manual workers be *more* resistant to feminist ideas than other men? Use evidence from extracts 3.18 and 3.19.

(b) Briefly outline the relationship between the sexes protrayed in the cartoon (3.20).

3.18

Spike (...) I've got the right bird, I've been goin' with her for eighteen months now. Her's as good as gold. She wouldn't look at another chap. She's fucking done well, she's clean. She loves doing fucking housework. Trousers I brought yesterday, I took 'em up last night, and her tuned 'em up for me(...) She's as good as gold and I wanna get married as soon as I can.

The model for the girlfriend is, of course, the mother and she is fundamentally a model of limitation. Though there is a great deal of affection for 'mum', she is definitely accorded an inferior role: 'She's a bit thick, like, never knows what I'm on about', 'She don't understand this sort of stuff, just me dad'. And within the home there is a clear sense that men have a right to be waited on by the mother.

[In an individual interview]

Spanksy (...) it shouldn't be done, you shouldn't need to help yer mother in the house. You should put your shoes away tidy and hang your coat up, admittedly, but, you know, you shouldn't vacuum and polish and do the beds for her and (...) her housekeeping and that.

Source: Paul Willis *Learning to Labour* (Gower, Farnborough, 1977)

3.19

'The Waggoner' is the focus of both male dominance and female subordination. Its ethos demonstrates the sexual antagonism that is embedded in the rural society's gender relations; it is an ethos saturated with male anxiety over female sexuality. Even though women, for the most part, are absent, their 'presence' dominates the discourse, in that the main topic of conversation in the pub is women's sexuality and the effective male control of it. Indeed, participating in 'nights out with the boys' is seen to reveal that they are real men, not under 'her' thumb; power must be seen to be held; 'I came down 'ere to 'ave a drink and a game of dominoes or darts or owt as is going on. I'm not like some buggers henpecked' (Quoted in Harrison 1943:131)

The geography of the pub is simple. There is a 'bottom' bar and a 'top' bar. Both are predominately male preserves, though women are invited into the 'top' bar at weekends or on special occasions. Whitehead (1976:175) provides a complete breakdown of the users of 'The Waggoner' in her analysis, but suffice it for me to say at this juncture that *women's* rights to engage in 'the licensed familiarity of the pub' are very restricted.

The clientele chiefly consists of male, semi-skilled labourers of low social status in comparison to the rest of the parish hierarchy. They occupy the 'bottom' bar and it is here that odd jobs are fixed up in a 'clearing house' where the lines between 'working' and 'drinking' become increasingly blurred (in more ways than one). This particular function of the pub, incidentally, provides a useful rationalization for men's continuous presence.

Source: Valerie Hey *Patriarchy and Pub Culture*, Tavistock, London, 1986

3.20

In direct contrast to the depressing passages above, the next two extracts, 3.21 and 3.22, are accounts of working class women taking a leading and active role in politics and in the conjugal relationship.
The women in the Women's Support Groups during the 1984–1985 miners' strike challenged the traditional 'male chauvinism' of the miners (3.21). In extract 3.22 we read of Phil and Wyn. He has lost status and authority as a result of becoming unemployed, and his wife has become both emotionally and economically dominant.

Using the evidence in extracts 3.21 and 3.22 explain what factors have enabled working class women to move away from their traditional role.

3.21

There is a long tradition and reputation for male chauvinism in Wales in general, and perhaps South Wales in particular. The extraordinary enterprise of the miners' wives during the strike left its mark on that tradition. Their activities were not universally welcomed by the men and even some of the older women had their doubts and reservations about getting too deeply involved in a 'man's world'. Picketing by the women was ruled out by most South Wales lodges. Yet nothing could prevent the wave of enthusiastic support and the organization skills the women displayed in running the food-supply network and in maintaining contacts with a national system of miners' aid groups.

Shirley James, wife of a striking miner and mother of a young unemployed son, claims that the experience of the dispute has transformed the lives of many women in miners' families throughout South Wales: 'Before the strike I was not interested in the union or in politics. I am now.'

Shirley James probably exemplifies how the miners' strike and the involvement of women from mining communities developed into a far broader social and poltical movement.

Before the strike I never thought about CND or nuclear weapons. But now I have been to Greenham Common and we've had people from France and Japan staying with us. Before the strike I believed what the papers said about the union and about the Greenham women. Things have changed.

Source: Geoffrey Goodman *The Miners' Strike* (Pluto Press, London, 1985)

3.22

There were also important changes in Wyn. We found her much stronger and more confident, now able to challenge Phil in front of others. She was obviously aware of the importance of her job and heartened by the fact that Phil had asked her to demand an increase in salary. She also felt justified in making complaints about Phil's poor performances as a housekeeper, all done in a semi-joking way. Although she had shelved the idea of a child more or less permanently, and more so now that they had found out that acromegaly was hereditary, Wyn's maternal needs were probably compensated in other ways. Phil had become more overtly dependent on her, and aware of his need for her care. These two roles, that of breadwinner and provider of health care, stengthened Wyn's self-esteem considerably, so she no longer saw herself as the weak member of the partnership. She realized that, under the circumstances, their survival depended on her being able to keep healthy and strong. Not surprisingly, she had not attended the general practitioner since November, and since then had been off all tranquilizers and anti-depressants.

Source: Fagin, L. and Little M. *The Forsaken Families* (Penguin, Harmondsworth, 1984)

Welsh miners' wives demonstrate in Birmingham, 1984

F. Was Marx Wrong?

Many Marxists to this day believe that the working class has the potential to play the crucial role in the creation of a socialist society. Extract 3.23 shows that this view is not all that popular in the modern Labour Party. Perhaps one of the reasons for this is provided in extract 3.24 which illustrates the declining size of the manual working class. The quotation from Margaret Thatcher suggests that not only Marxism, but the whole concept of class, is irrelevant in Britain today.

(a) Using extracts 3.23 and 3.24, suggest what sort of policies Mr. Gould might be in favour of and which he might oppose.

(b) Briefly comment on Mrs Thatcher's view of a classless Britain (3.25).

3.23

Male Occupations (%)

	1911	1951	1971
Managerial/professional	6.9	12.6	21.5
Intermediate occupations	11.9	13.3	14.5
Manual working class	73.6	68.4	58.8

Goldthorpe, J.H. et al. *Social Mobility and Class Structure in Modern Britain* (Clarendon Press, Oxford, 1980)

3.24

Does the old working class still exist? These days in the Labour Party, it sometimes seems that the only person who thinks so is Tony Benn; and even he only talks about 'working-people'.

The party leaders rarely use either phrase. They dress and talk as if the last thing they want is for people to get the idea that Labour is a working-class party. The man of the moment, Mr Bryan Gould, MP, seems particularly intent on distancing himself from any hint of cloth-cap politics, both by the natty, marketing man image he presents and by what he says. He evidently believes that the way for Labour to win the next election is to forget the cloth caps and to target instead the affluent Sainsbury trolley working class of the new estates and new service economy of the South.

Source. 'View of the Workers' *The Observer* 19.9.87

3.25

Margaret Thatcher (19.3.88) defending the tax concessions to the rich in the budget of March, 1988

But others, and not only Marxists, caution us about believing that class or class struggle are dead. Extracts 3.26–3.28 support the view that social inequality and class conflict are still important and real features of modern Britian.

ACTIVITY 12
Using extracts 3.26–3.28 write a newspaper article of around 250 words entitled 'Class is not Dead'.

3.26

In point of fact there is a class struggle every day in every factory. Maybe it is rarely consciously thought of as a class struggle but it is exactly that. Managements are constantly trying to increase production, to keep down wage costs and to use labour in what appear to managements to be the most efficient manner . . . Workers must constantly try to prevent the pace of work becoming too oppressive and struggle to ensure that real earnings are edged up rather than down. As with managements, exactly what this means must depend upon the situation. It may involve fooling the work-study man, bargaining over bonuses and piece-rates or getting control over the speed of the assembly line.

Far from the class war being dead, all these are daily issues throughout industry.

Source: K. Roberts *et al. The Fragmentary Class Structure* (Heinemann, London, 1977).

3.27

It is necessary to challenge not only the conventional wisdom that insists that the working class is disappearing because less than a third of all workers are now employed in manufacturing industry, but also those Marxist formulations which declare that sellers of labour-power remain doomed to discover the true nature of their situation. Thus, even as the 'traditional' working class shrinks from year to year, so that coal miners, for instance, now constitute one tenth of their number fifty years ago, it is constantly being augmented by new categories of worker which capitalism is calling into existence. This is happening with the reconstitution of large sections of the working class in the interest of 'service industries' that new and unfamiliar manifestation of something age-old, a subordination that descends directly from that of those unfortunate people called to be hired annually at the Michaelmas mop as farm servants, or to be carried off into the Victorian suburbs as little more than children to scour the steps and polish the brass and blacklead the grate in rambling redbrick villas.

Source: Trevor Blackwell and Jeremy Seabrook *A World Still to Win* (Faber & Faber, London, 1985)

3.28

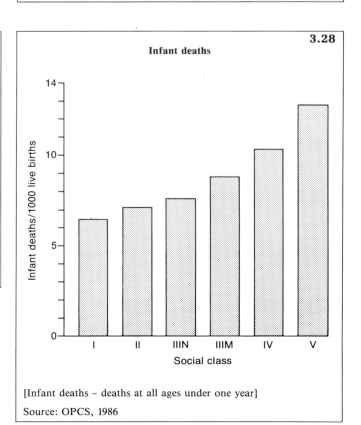

Infant deaths

[Infant deaths – deaths at all ages under one year]

Source: OPCS, 1986

Conclusion

The sociology of the working class is a minefield for the unsuspecting student – a mass of contradictory evidence at the centre of a heated debate. The evidence supplied in this chapter has been selected to provide support for an admittedly over simple argument, but one which is worth restating.

The story of the working class has been one of change. A traditional, geographically and socially immobile and relatively homogeneous working class, living in old communities with fairly distinct values (and all quite easily romanticised) existed in the early part of this century, and still exists, perhaps, in pockets where older industries survive. But mobility, re-housing and affluence for some, created a new more affluent worker. Ideas of community and solidarity (and masculinity) have been partly replaced by a privatised, fragmented and less traditional working class – a division well illustrated by the difference between home owners and council tenants. In an extreme version of this argument, 'capitalist' values have replaced more communal or even socialist values.

This diversity of the working class has been added to by the arrival of new recruits, ethnic minorities, waged women, the unemployed, service workers. And added to these changes is at least the beginning of a breakdown in old, sexist, male working class attitudes.

Now is the time to return to the quotes at the beginning of the chapter. Using the evidence presented in this chapter and any other sociological knowledge and understanding you have, try to see which side you come down on in the final activity.

ACTIVITY 13

Divide a page into two colums and write *The Working Class* as a heading. Put 'Evidence for Dahrendorf' at the top of one column and 'Evidence for Marx' at the top of the other.

In the Dahrendorf column write down a list of evidence from this chapter and elsewhere which supports the view that the working class is no longer a distinct social group. In the Marxist column do the same to support the view that the working class is still important and distinct.

Write a paragraph in which you state your view on this issue (you do not have to agree with either Marx or Dahrendorf).

3.29

'The proletarians have nothing to lose but their chains. They have a world to win.' Marx and Engels *The Communist Manifesto*, 1848

'. . . it has become doubtful whether speaking of the working class still makes much sense.' Ralf Dahrendorf *Class and Class Conflict in Industrial Society*, 1959.

Further reading

Goodman, G. *The Miners' Strike*, Pluto Press, London, 1985
Marshall, G. 'What is Happening to the Working Class?' *Social Studies Review* Vol. 2, No. 3
Pryce, K. *Endless Pressure*, Penguin, Harmondsworth, 1979
Roberts, K. *et al. The Fragmentary Class Structure* Heinemann, London, 1977
Seabrook, J. *Working Class Childhood* Victor Gollancz, London, 1982

UNIT 4 Why do the Conservatives keep winning General Elections?

This unit examines reasons for the success of the Conservative Party in the General Elections of 1979, 1983 and 1987. It considers the short term factors and the wider social changes which led to these victories.

Introduction

At a General Election the country is divided into 650 constituencies (the number has increased since 1945). Each constituency consists of about 70,000 voters, all at least 18 years old, and these elect one Member of Parliament to the House of Commons. The party with the most MP's forms the government. The results of all the elections since the end of the Second World War are given in table 4.1.

ACTIVITY 1

(a) List the main factors which you think would influence the result of a General Election.

(b) Indicate their order of importance.

4.1

General Election results

1945	Labour
1950	Labour
1951	Conservative
1955	Conservative
1959	Conservative
1964	Labour
1966	Labour
1970	Conservative
Feb 1974	Labour
Oct 1974	Labour
1979	Conservative
1983	Conservative
1987	Conservative

Short term factors

In your list of influential factors you may have 'policies', or something like it. Policies are bound to influence election results. Labour's commitment to unilateral nuclear disarmament in 1983 and 1987 was widely felt to have damaged their electoral chances. Similarly, a government can make such a mess of running the country, or have such bad luck that the electorate blame it and vote for the opposition. This happened during the strike-torn 'winter of discontent' in 1978–79 which helped to unseat the Labour government. Because policy changes occur even within the space of a few years they can be called 'short term' factors in influencing election results.

ACTIVITY 2

(a) What do extracts 4.2, 4.3 and 4.4 tell us about the importance of policies?

(b) Where would you now place 'policies' in your list from Activity 1?

4.2

The concentration of much of the (Labour) campaign upon the state of the health and education services reflected a change in mood among the electorate . . . *British Social Attitudes 1987* has shown a clear trend away from the Conservative position on a number of key matters since 1983. The welfare state has become more popular. Tax cuts are less popular and redistribution of income and wealth more popular, privatisation less popular.

Source: 'Must Labour Lose?' J. Curtice *New Society*, 19 June, 1987

4.3

In the 1987 Election the four most salient issues were unemployment, the National Health Service, education and defence. Professor Ivor Crewe commented that 'had electors voted on the main issues Labour would have won' because, according to opinion polls, Labour was seen as the most competent on unemployment, the NHS and education, with the Conservatives seen as the most competent on defence.

Source: *Sociology Update 1988* M. Denscombe, Hyperion Press, Leicester

4.4

'*Under the Tories the welfare state's been run down, unemployment's rocketed and the nationalised industries have been sold off for a song... They've certainly got my vote.*'

Another short term factor is the quality of the party leaders. In the 1987 General Election both the main party leaders had what Max Weber called *charisma*, or exceptional powers of leadership. Perhaps this affected the election result.

ACTIVITY 3

(a) What qualities do you think leaders need to have if they are to be called 'charismatic'? Do any politicians you know of possess these qualities?

(b) Looking at data 4.5–4.7 suggest how a politician might improve his or her image as a strong leader?

(c) Using data 4.5 to 4.8, say what impact you think 'leadership' had on the 1987 election result. (Mrs Thatcher was returned to office with a parliamentary majority of 101 – a 'landslide' victory.)

4.5

4.6

4.7

As Kinnock neared the end of an hour there was a hint of restlessness among the delegates seated in the raked auditorium of the brand-new conference centre on the cliffs just west of Bournemouth's town centre. That was the point at which he eventually broached the theme of extremism and impossibilism, beginning with a vivid portrayal of how impossible promises came to be made and what happened to people foolish enought to believe them:

You start with far-fetched resolutions. They are then pickled into a rigid dogma, a code, and you go through the years sticking to that, out-dated, misplaced, irrelevant to the real needs, and you end in the grotesque chaos...

– now he was raising his voice until he was nearly shouting, and excited murmurs were already rippling through the hall –

...the grotesque chaos of a Labour council – a *Labour* council – hiring taxis [he almost spat the word] to scuttle around a city handing out redundancy notices to its own workers

Source: *Kinnock*, M. Leapman, Unwin Hyman, London, 1987

4.8

Q: Regardless of how you voted today, which of the party leaders do you think came across best during the campaign?

	All voters	Con voters	Lab voters	SDP/Lib voters
Margaret Thatcher	37	71	8	18
Neil Kinnock	40	14	80	31
David Owen	12	8	4	31
David Steel	6	3	4	16

Source: ITN/Harris Exit Poll, *The Independent* June 15 1987

Voters' perceptions of parties and leaders depend partly on how the latter are presented in the mass media. Sociologists, therefore, must ask the question; is the media a 'window on the world' or does it present politics though blue tinted spectacles? The following data suggest that most newspapers are biased against the Labour party.

ACTIVITY 4

(a) Why might 'coverage of London councils be particularly inaccurate and distorted in... *The Sun, Daily Mail, Mail on Sunday* and *London Evening Standard*'?

(b) Why might the 'Baa Baa Black Sheep' story appeal to the readership of the newspapers which printed it?

(c) Why do you think so many newspapers support the Conservative Party?

4.9

NOW IT'S BAA BAA BLANK SHEEP

'Racist' Rhyme Banned

Source: *Daily Star* 15.2.86

4.10

WHO OWNS WHAT		
The Big 5 Newspaper Proprietors		
Owner	Papers Owned	Party Supported
Pergamon Press	Daily Mirror Sunday Mirror Sunday People	Labour
Fleet Holdings	Daily Express Daily Star Sunday Express	Conservative
Associated Newspapers	Daily Mail Mail on Sunday	Conservative
News International	The Sun The Times The News of the World The Sunday Times	Conservative
Telegraph Newspaper Trust	Daily Telegraph Sunday Telegraph	Conservative

Source: adapted from 'New Society Database – The Press', *New Society*, 28.11.86

4.11

The story which has come to encapsulate the tabloid image of the "loony left" was the alleged banning of the nursery rhyme Baa Baa Black Sheep. The story appears to have surfaced originally in the Daily Star (February 15, 1986), which claimed that Beavers Play Group in Hackney had suppressed the rhyme. This was reworked by the Sun (February 20, 1985) into "loony left-wing councillors have banned children from reciting the nursery rhyme."

In fact, the council had not banned the rhyme. All that happened is that the parent-run Beavers Play Group had sometimes sung a humorous alternative version of the rhyme, beginning "Baa Baa White Sheep..." and ending "and one for the little boy (or girl) with holes in his (her) socks," as well as singing the conventional version of the rhyme.

The story was given a new twist by Anthony Doran in the Daily Mail (October 9, 1986), who reported that Haringey council had banned the rhyme at a racism awareness course which play leaders in the borough had been instructed to attend. This report was repeated in a large number of other papers. In fact, the council issued no such ban. It is not even clear that the rhyme was even discussed at the racism course, where attendance was voluntary.

Out of all the papers which repeated the story, only the Yorkshire Evening Press had the grace to print a retraction, acknowledging that it had relied on "an inaccurate report."

Coverage of London councils has been particularly inaccurate and distorted in four papers – The Sun, Daily Mail, Mail on Sunday and the London Evening Standard. Their more lurid and misleading reports on "loony left" authorities have been regularly repeated in local newspapers up and down the country. They have also been incorporated into briefings issued by the Conservative Party Central Office.

Source: *Media Coverage of London Council – Interim Report*, Media Research Group, Goldsmiths College, London, 1987

It is accepted that newspapers will represent particular political viewpoints. However, television is obliged to show 'due impartiality'. Nevertheless, some sociological research, notably the work of the Glasgow Media Group, has suggested that television puts across a 'pro-establishment' view.

ACTIVITY 5

(a) What point do you think the cartoonist is making in data 4.13?

(b) Data 4.14 is an excerpt from the transcript of a TV interview with Michael Foot, then the leader of the Labour Party.
  (i) What assumptions does the interviewer hold about the Labour Party?
  (ii) How might this affect the viewer's image of the Labour Party?

(c) Consider data 4.13 and 4.14 in the light of the 'due impartiality' outlined in data 4.12

4.12

It should be the duty of the Authority to satisfy themselves that so far as possible the programmes broadcast by the Authority comply with the following requirements: That is to say . . . that due impartiality is preserved on the part of persons providing the programmes as respects matters of political or industrial controversy or relating to current public policy.

(IBA Act 1973)

The licence requires the BBC to refrain from editorialising

(BBC Handbook 1977)

4.13

'And to ensure a balanced and impartial discussion of the latest government measures, I have with me a government spokesman and a wild-eyed Trot from the lunatic fringe.'

Source: *Really Bad News*, Glasgow Media Group, Writers and Readers, London, 1982

4.14

(1) INTERVIEWER: (Are you) a bridge builder, a peacemaker inside the party?
FOOT: Well yes, but not a caretaker . . .

(2) INTERVIEWER: Are you the sort of man who can be *pushed about by the left* inside the party if they pushed you into standing against your will?
FOOT: They didn't push me into standing against my will . . .

Source: *News at Ten*, 30.10.80
(reprinted in *Really Bad News*, Glasgow Media Group, Writers and Readers, London, 1982)

It needs to be added, however, that television coverage of current affairs has not only been criticised by supporters of the 'left'. Norman Tebbit, when Chairman of the Conservative party, made several complaints to the BBC about anti-government bias in their coverage.

ACTIVITY 6

(a) Put Katz's arguments (4.15) into your own words.

(b) What reassurance do you think Katz would be able to offer those in the Labour Party who were critical of mass media coverage of their campaign?

4.15

The media and the voters: a summary of effects research

- Despite the many differences among countries and from election to election, typically about 80 per cent, or more, of the voters have made up their minds about their vote before the campaign begins, that is at least several months prior to the election . . .
- More than the mass media are able to convert, they reinforce vote intentions and the basic loyalties underlying them . . . Those who are 'seeking reinforcement' are more politically interested, and more politically sophisticated. They are more selective in their viewing, and are often looking for ammunition for political arguments with others. They use the media to help adjust their political attitudes to those articulated by their party.
- Sometimes, as certain studies show, the media influence votes indirectly by focusing on an issue which, in turn, affects the frame of reference of the 'guidance seekers', and perhaps others . . .

Source: adapted from 'Platforms and Windows – Broadcasting's Role in Election Campaigns', E. Katz in *The Sociology of Mass Communications* edited by D. McQuail, Penguin, Harmondsworth, 1972.

Although the power of the media to influence voters in the short term is limited, the final point in data 4.15 suggests that, over longer periods, the mass media can select the kinds of issues which are brought to the public's attention and the 'frame of reference' in which they are understood. Other less obvious factors are also very important in affecting election results over the long term.

Long term factors

ACTIVITY 7

(a) Draw a graph or bar chart to show changes in the main parties percentage share of the vote during the period covered by the table (4.16).

(b) What has happened to support for the third party and how has this affected support for the main parties?

4.16

Date	Party	Number of votes (millions)	Percentage of Votes
Feb 1974	Conservative	11.9	37.9
	Labour	11.6	37.1
	Liberal	6.1	19.3
	Others	1.8	5.6
Oct 1974	Conservative	10.5	35.8
	Labour	11.5	39.2
	Liberal	5.3	18.3
	Others	1.9	6.6
1979	Conservative	13.7	43.9
	Labour	11.5	36.9
	Liberal	4.3	13.8
	Others	1.7	5.5
1983	Conservative	13.0	42.4
	Labour	8.5	27.6
	Liberal	7.8	25.4
	Others	1.4	4.6
1987	Conservative	13.7	42.3
	Labour	10.0	30.8
	Liberal	7.3	22.6
	Others	1.3	4.3

ACTIVITY 8

(a) What is the relationship between region and voting patterns?

(b) What explanations can you give for the difference in voting patterns between the South East and Wales?

(c) Northern Ireland does not exhibit the same voting patterns as other areas of economic depression. Why do you think this is?

4.17

Regional performance. Ranked by gdp per head.

	Gdp per head 1985	Personal disposable income per head, 1985	Real personal disposable income growth per head, 1975-85	Unemployment % of working population Jan 1987	Long term unemployed % of unemployed Jan 1987
South East	5831	4725	19.92	8.5	36.2
East Anglia	5118	4244	26.21	9.3	33.5
Scotland	4942	4181	20.86	15.1	39.2
North West	4877	4074	16.95	14.3	44.3
E. Midlands	4861	4066	18.46	11.4	39.2
South West	4763	4152	21.34	10.4	32.7
North	4717	3919	18.24	16.9	44.3
W. Midlands	4690	3997	10.24	13.8	46.3
Yorks & Humb	4662	3923	17.70	13.8	42.0
Wales	4509	3778	14.27	14.3	40.6
N. Ireland	3799	3538	18.67	19.3	50.0

Source: Economic Trends, Employment Gazette.

Source: *Lloyds Bank Economic Bulletin*, May 1987

4.18

Share of the vote in the 1987 General Election

Orkney Islands Shetland Islands

Scotland

North

Yorkshire and Humberside

North West

East Midlands

West Midlands

Wales

East Anglia

South East

South West

BRITAIN

	% of vote	Change on '83	Seats
CON	43.3	−0.2	375
LAB	31.5	+3.2	229
ALL	23.1	−3.0	22
NAT	1.7	+0.2	6

NORTH

	% of vote	Change on '83	Seats
CON	32.0	−2.3	8
LAB	47.0	+7.1	27
ALL	20.8	−4.0	1

NORTH WEST

	% of vote	Change on '83	Seats
CON	38.0	−2.0	34
LAB	41.2	+5.2	36
ALL	20.6	−3.0	3

WEST MIDLANDS

	% of vote	Change on '83	Seats
CON	45.5	+0.6	36
LAB	33.3	+2.1	22
ALL	20.8	−2.6	0

WALES

	% of vote	Change on '83	Seats
CON	29.5	−1.5	8
LAB	45.1	+7.5	24
ALL	17.9	−5.3	3
NAT	7.3	−0.5	3

SOUTH WEST

	% of vote	Change on '83	Seats
CON	50.6	−0.8	44
LAB	16.2	+1.5	1
ALL	32.8	−0.4	3

SCOTLAND

	% of vote	Change on '83	Seats
CON	24.0	−4.4	10
LAB	42.4	+7.3	50
ALL	19.2	−5.3	9
SNP	14.0	+2.3	3

YORKS & HUMBERSIDE

	% of vote	Change on '83	Seats
CON	37.4	−1.2	21
LAB	40.6	+5.3	33
ALL	21.7	−3.9	0

EAST MIDLANDS

	% of vote	Change on '83	Seats
CON	48.6	+1.4	31
LAB	30.0	+2.1	11
ALL	21.0	−3.1	0

EAST ANGLIA

	% of vote	Change on '83	Seats
CON	52.1	+1.2	19
LAB	21.7	+1.2	1
ALL	25.8	−2.5	0

GREATER LONDON

	% of vote	Change on '83	Seats
CON	46.5	+2.6	58
LAB	31.5	+1.6	23
ALL	21.3	−3.5	3

SOUTH EAST

	% of vote	Change on '83	Seats
CON	55.8	+1.1	107
LAB	16.8	+0.9	1
ALL	26.9	−1.8	0

'The Party of One Nation'? The Conservatives' share of the vote in Scotland, Wales and the English regions:

Less than 25%; 25%–30%; 30%–35%; 35%–40%; 45%–50%; 50%–55%; over 55%.

Note: The share of the vote of 'others' is not shown, so figures in each box do not total 100% and plus and minus changes figures do not necessarily tally

Source: *Social Studies Review*, Vol. 3, No. 1, Sept. 1987

Alignment

One conclusion you may have reached from Activity 8 is that there is a relationship between affluence and voting behaviour. There clearly is a 'fit' or 'alignment' between the two main parties and the middle and working class. In fact, some people have said that 'class is party'. The following evidence shows why.

ACTIVITY 9

(a) Using data 4.19, describe the relationship between the social class of the voter and the party voted for.

(b) The figures in data 4.19 are incomplete in order to exaggerate the extent of 'alignment'. What is missing?

(c) Using data 4.20–4.25
    (i) Why do you think that the middle class tends to favour the Conservative Party?
    (ii) Why do you think that the working class appears to favour the Labour Party?

4.19

		Middle class (A,B) [%]	Semi and Unskilled Working class (D,E) [%]
Conservative	1973	67	25
	1983	62	29
	1987	59	31
Labour	1973	10	54
	1983	12	44
	1987	14	50

Source: adapted from *Introduction to British Politics*, P. Madgwick, 3rd edition, Hutchinson, London, 1988 and 'A New Class of Politics', Ivor Crewe, *The Guardian*, 15.6.87

4.20

Mrs Thatcher with multi-millionaire Charles Forte at the official opening of his new motorway services on the M25 in 1987

4.21

On the march for jobs, marking the 50th anniversary of the original 1936 march from Jarrow.

4.22

Conservative Party Manifesto, 1987

We have:

reduced sharply the absurd top rates of tax inherited from Labour which were causing so many of our most talented people to work abroad;

increased greatly the tax relief for charitable donations. Giving to charities has doubled since we first took office;

abolished four taxes completely: the national insurance surcharge – the tax which Labour put on jobs – the investment income surcharge, the development land tax and the lifetime gifts tax;

reformed and simplified corporation tax, and cut its rate to the lowest of any major industrial country;

cut the small business corporation tax rate by more than a third, and extended it to many more small businesses;

reformed and reduced capital taxes as well as slashing stamp duty.

4.23

Labour Party Manifesto, 1987

We are determined to make Britain a fairer and freer society:

To us and to the majority of the British people a civilised community is one in which citizens band together to provide, out of community resources to which all contribute, essential services like health, education and pensions that the great majority of people cannot afford to provide for themselves at a time of need.

When the Tories talk of freedom, they mean freedom for the few, for those who can afford to buy privilege. What they mean, as their record so plainly shows, is more tax cuts for the rich and less help for the poor and for the great majority who are neither rich nor poor.

Labour's objective is to broaden and deepen the liberty of all individuals in our community: to free people from poverty, exploitation and fear; to free them to realise their full potential; to see that everyone has the liberty to enjoy real chances, to make real choices.

4.24		
The social background of Members of Parliament (1979)		
	Conservative	Labour
Lawyers	21	7
Manual workers	0.9	31
Public School	73	17
Teachers	5	21
Source: Madgwick, *op. cit*.		

4.25

The trade unions are the basis of the Labour Party. Historically they created it in the famous decision of 1900 to set up a Labour representation committee. Constitutionally, through political affiliation, the unions provide the bulk of the membership, great majority in conference and over half the National Executive Committee...they sponsor about two-fifths of Labour MPs.

Source: Madgwick, *op. cit*.

The evidence you have looked at so far might lead you to believe that the social class dominates voting behaviour. Factors like policies, leaders and campaigns are all obscured by the determining facts that 'class *is* party'. Although in Britain class is still a very important influence on the way people vote, the situation in the last quarter of a century has become a lot more complicated.

Firstly, the size of the social classes is changing.

ACTIVITY 10

(a) Describe the main trends in data 4.26

(b) What view of the Labour voter does Neil Kinnock see as 'politically immature'?

(c) How could he use figures to support his argument?

4.26

Class composition of the electorate [%]		
	1964	1983
Salariat	18	27
Routine NM	18	24
Petty Bourgeoisie	7	8
Foremen/Technicians	10	7
Working class	47	34

(for an explanation of these categories, see data 4.31)

Source: *How Britain Votes*, A. Heath, R. Jowell and J. Curtice, Pergamon Press, Oxford 1983

4.27

The idea that there is a model Labour voter, a blue collar council house tenant who belongs to a union and has 2.4 children, a five year old car and a holiday in Blackpool, is patronising and politically immature...The idea that a vague coalition of 'have nots' can be built as an adequate base for Labour support and that therefore no effort is needed to secure the backing of the 'haves' and the 'haven't got enoughs' is a betrayal of the very people that we most want to help by gaining and using democratic power.

Neil Kinnock, May 1986

4.28

...in late capitalism it is not so much the state as the working class that appears to be withering away. A majority of the working population is now in white collar occupations...the working class fell from just under one half of the electorate in 1964 to little more than one third in 1983.

Source: 'Must Labour Lose' J. Curtice, *New Society*, 19 June 1987

Dealignment

But the remaining members of the working class are far from solid Labour voters. The recent sociological debate about working class voting behaviour can be traced back to 1959 when Labour suffered its third successive electoral defeat. In *Must Labour Lose?* Abrams saw increasing working class affluence as the main reason for Labour's failure. In fact, Labour went on to hold office for 11 of the 15 years following the 1964 election.

Today, in the wake of a further three successive Conservative victories, arguments not unlike the 'embourgeoisement' thesis (see Unit 3) are being used to explain Labour's failure. This has resulted in some quite heated controversy about whether or not Labour's class base is breaking up. The main protagonists are the political scientist Ivor Crewe on the one hand and, on the other, Heath, Jowell, and Curtice whose book *How Britain Votes* (Pergamon, Oxford, 1983) challenged some of Crewe's arguments.

Working class divisions and voting behaviour 1983 and 1987

ACTIVITY 11
Using data 4.29–4.30

(a) What divisions in the working class does Crewe describe?

(b) How is Heath, Jowell, and Curtice's classification of the working class different?

(c) According to Crewe, which sections of the working class have deserted Labour? Why do you think this is?

(d) Using Heath, Jowell, and Curtice's classification, what effect does removing 'foremen and technicians' appear to have on working class support for Labour?

(e) Crewe argues that 'dealignment' is occurring: class is becoming a less significant influence on voting behaviour. Using data 4.29, what 'new' divisions does Crewe believe are becoming more important?

(f) Crewe argues that 'the picture is even gloomier for Labour this time' (data 4.29) and Curtice that 'Labour is in serious difficulties' (data 4.30). Explain why each writer argues this.

4.29

Ivor Crewe
1987 General Election

THE TRADITIONAL WORKING CLASS

	Lives in Scotland/North	Council tenant	Union member	Works in public sector
Con	29	25	30	32
Lab	57	57	48	49
Lib/SDP	15	18	22	19

THE NEW WORKING CLASS

	Lives in South	owner-occupier	Non-union	works in private sector
Con	46	44	40	38
Lab	28	32	38	39
Lib/SDP	26	24	22	23

In one important sense the picture is even gloomier for Labour this time. Government policies are producing a steady expansion of the new working class, and diminution of the old. Council house sales, privatisation, the decline of manufacturing industry (on which the old unions are based) and the steady population drift to the South have re-structured the working class. The new working class is not only the dominant segment but increasingly dominant. Demography and time are not on Labour's side. Its need to break out of its old class fortresses is more urgent than ever but on present evidence no nearer in sight.

Labour partly remobilised the "rank and file" working class of semi and unskilled manual workers, among whom its vote rose by a full six percentage points, twice the national average. But it failed spectacularly in the other half of the working class, the "NCOs" of foremen, supervisors, craft and high-tech workers who make up the market researchers' "C2" category of "skilled manual workers." Here there was a further swing to the Conservatives of 2.5 per cent since 1983.

Source: Crewe, op. cit.

4.30

Heath, Jowell, and Curtice

Must Labour lose?

There is a sharp distinction to be drawn between this account of the role of economic prosperity in how people vote and that of the embourgeoisement thesis. The latter implies a permanent shift of behaviour among a specific section of the electorate. The account given here argues that economic optimism is a short-term influence upon behaviour which affects the electorate as a whole and its continued benefit to the Conservatives is dependent upon the continued good management of the economy. It does not necessarily imply a Conservative hegemony into the 21st century.

Labour is in serious difficulties. In the absence of an ability to carve out a new electoral base for itself, social change is making its prospects of winning office even more remote. But the influence of socioeconomic position upon voting behaviour is not so inexorable that its influence cannot be counteracted. Britain still has a competitive party system; it is possible to envisage that the Conservatives could lose their overall majority at the next election. But Britain no longer has a system of alternating two-party politics.

Source: Curtice, op. cit.

1. **The salariat:** managers, professionals, semi-professionals and non-manual supervisors.
2. **Routine non-manual:** clerks, sales assistants, secretaries.
3. **Petty bourgeoisie:** self-employed small business people.
4. **Foremen and technicians:** supervisors of manual workers, a 'blue collar elite'.
5. **The working class:** all 'rank and file' manual employees, skilled and unskilled.

Social class and party support, 1983

	Con	Lab	SDP/LIB
Salariat	54	14	31
Routine non-manual	46	25	27
Petty bourgeoisie	71	12	17
Foremen	48	26	25
Working class	30	49	20

Source: Heath, Jowell and Curtice op. cit.

Some parts of the argument put forward by Heath, Jowell, and Curtice are reminiscent of earlier accounts of voting behaviour. In 1972 for instance, McKenzie and Silver termed some working class Conservatives 'secular' voters. These people voted Conservative because they believed that Conservative policies would most benefit them personally. Goldthorpe and Lockwood's famous study of 'affluent workers' found that a substantial proportion of their sample voted Labour for similarly 'instrumental' reasons.

ACTIVITY 12

(a) Why do you think that 'as part of its contribution to the Conservative cause' the *Sun* focused on the issues it did? (data 4.31)

(b) In the light of the comments above, and data 4.31 and 4.32, why do you think that Curtice (data 4.30) argues that their findings 'do not necessarily imply a Conservative hegemony (leadership) into the 21st century'?

4.31

As part of its contribution to the Conservative cause, the *Sun* has invited its readers to confide how much profit they have made in twelve months from the purchase of their council house: the record of £50,000, briefly held by a tiler from Nottingham, was easily broken two days later, as a man from Purley boasted a gain of £76,000. The paper also carried a feature on why Britain's blacks should vote Tory, by coloured (sic) candidate, John Taylor. It also gave prominence to the lives of smoked-salmon socialists—fine-living fat cats, with a picture of Denis Healey's "£500,000 mansion in one of Britain's prettiest villages;" and silver-spoon lefties—"Tony Benn who owns a £750,000 castle. Harriet Harman, on the other hand, "tries to conceal her plummy accent." The article concludes "Most Labour MPs are as interested in personal gain as the rest of us—though they hate to admit it." This view is echoed by Jean Rook in the *Express* who, though bored with politics, will "vote for the party most likely to aid me personally to grab all I can get."

Source: 'What the Papers Show', J. Seabrook, *New Society*, 5.6.87

4.32

My heart tells me to vote Labour, my head tells me to vote SDP/Liberal, but my wallet tells me to vote Conservative (Mick Jagger, 1987)

ACTIVITY 13

You have been commissioned by one of the main political parties. Using all the evidence and arguments you have been introduced to in this unit, write a paper for *either* the Conservative *or* the Labour Party advising them on election strategy in the 1990s.

Further Reading

Benyon, J. 'A prolonged Conservative ascendancy in a divided Britain?' *Social Studies Review* Vol. 3, No. 1, 1987

Crewe, I. 'Why Mrs Thatcher was returned with a landslide' *Social Studies Review*, Vol. 3, No. 1, 1987

Curtice, J. 'Must Labour Lose' *New Society* 19.6.87

Heath, A., Jowell, R., Curtice, J. *How Britain Votes* Pergamon, Oxford, 1983

Jowell, R., Witherspoon, S., Brook, L. *British Social Attitudes, 1987,* Gower, Aldershot, 1987 (Chapters 3 and 8)

UNIT 5 Defining and Measuring Poverty

> 'Want, in the sense of absolute deprivation, has been largely eliminated.'
> (Green paper on Social Security Reform 1985)
>
> 'The past five years have witnessed a high-water mark in the rising tide of poverty'.
> (Pond, C. and Burghes, L. 'The Rising Tide of Deprivation', *New Society*, 18.4.86)

Introduction

At first reading, these two statements seem to contradict each other. In this unit, the intention is to clarify whether they are, in fact, contradictory. If they are, then which one is correct? If they are not, then how can they be reconciled with each other?

We cannot, of course, answer these questions without clarifying what it is that we are talking about. As in any sociological discussion, it is necessary first to establish a definition of what is being discussed – in this case, **poverty**.

Defining poverty

Seebohm Rowntree was born in 1871 into a wealthy Liberal Quaker family. He believed that it was the responsibility of the state to lay down minimum standards of living and to protect citizens from falling beneath them. In 1899 he carried out a survey of the working class population of York, to find out what proportion of the population was living in poverty, and what the causes were. In order to head off criticism that his definition might be too generous, he deliberately defined poverty at the lowest possible level.

ACTIVITY 1

(a) Picture a family, consisting of husband, wife and three children at the turn of the century. They are living in secondary poverty because part of their income was spent on some of the activities listed in the last paragraph of extract 5.1. Would you consider their spending on these items in Rowntree's words to be 'useful or wasteful'? Give reasons for your answer.

(b) From your point of view:
  (i) Should secondary poverty count as poverty?
  (ii) Should those in secondary poverty receive assistance from the state?
  Give reasons for your answers.

5.1

Families regarded as living in poverty were grouped under two heads:

(a) Families whose total earnings were insufficient to obtain the minimum necessaries for the maintenance of merely physical efficiency. Poverty falling under this head was described as 'primary' poverty;

(b) Families whose total earnings would have been sufficient for the maintenance of merely physical efficiency were it not that some portion of it was absorbed by other expenditure, either useful or wasteful. Poverty falling under this head was described as 'secondary' poverty.

And let us clearly understand what 'merely physical efficiency' means: a family living upon the scale allowed for must never spend a penny on railway fare or omnibus. They must never go into the country unless they walk. They must never purchase a halfpenny newspaper or spend a penny to buy a ticket for a popular concert. They must write no letters to absent children, for they cannot afford to pay the postage. They must never contribute anything to their church or chapel, or give any help to a neighbour which costs them money. They cannot save nor can they join a sick club or trade union, because they cannot pay the necessary subscriptions. The children must have no pocket money for dolls, marbles or sweets. The father must smoke no tobacco and drink no beer. The mother must never buy any pretty clothes for herself or her children, the character of the family wardrobe, as for the family diet, being governed by the regulation 'nothing must be bought but that which is absolutely necessary for the maintenance of physical health and what is bought must be of the plainest and most economical description'.

Source: *Poverty: A Study of Town Life* S. Rowntree, Macmillan, London, 1901

5.2

To calculate his standard of 'merely physical efficiency', Rowntree first made a list of the basic necessities of life. He asked experts to devise a week's diet for a family of specified size, combining adequate nutrition-value with minimum cost. He then costed this at current prices. To these food costs, he added the cost of clothing, of household sundries, of fuel and light, and of personal sundries. Rent was priced separately.

Rowntree updated this price-list, and added some additional items, in his two subsequent surveys, published in 1941 and 1951. In 1950, he calculated that a total weekly subsistence-level income for a married couple with three children (excluding rent) was £5 0s 2d. Obviously, inflation has meant that this figure would now be much higher.

Rowntree's method of calculation was used by William Beveridge when he devised the first National Assistance Board scales in the 1940s. 'My primary poverty line...was bare standard of subsistence rather than living...such a minimum does not by any means constitute a reasonable living wage.' (Beveridge, 1942).

The Rowntree/Beveridge principles underlie the Supplementary Benefit scales (replaced by Income Support in April 1988).

In Britain in 1987, Supplementary Benefit (SB) was payable to those whose **resources** (their actual income plus their savings) were less than their **requirements** (as calculated at the current official rates, with housing costs calculated separately).

Data 5.3 gives an example of a family's Supplementary Benefit situation in April 1987. Data 5.4 gives details of Income Support for April 1988.

ACTIVITY 2

(a) What are the basic needs of a married couple, with two children under five, living in a city in Britain today? What income do they need to meet these needs?

To calculate this, you will have to list their areas of expenditure (e.g. food, clothing, fuel and light, household sundries, personal sundries) and then to list their weekly purchases and bills under these headings. Then go to the shops and cost them at today's prices. You need to stick to Rowntree's strict subsistence level, but you should include only what you think are the bare necessities for this family.

(b) How do the requirement figures in data 5.3 compare with your own calculation of needs?

(c) Assuming that Supplementary Benefits brought this family's income up to the level of their official requirements (i.e. £72.35 plus rent/mortgage payments), how would you describe their situation on SB in Britain in 1987? Poor? Deprived? Badly off? Adequately supplied? At a reasonable standard?

(d) Imagine this family living in a large city in Britain today. How would they spend their time? What leisure activities would be available to them? What would their social life be like? How much would they be able to participate in the life of their community?

(e) How will this family's economic situation change as the children get older and start school?

5.3
State benefits

You are an unemployed, married man with a non-earning wife and two children under five. You are a council tenant and pay rent and rates (including water rates) of £27.00 a week. Your requirements would be as follows:

Weekly scale rate for married couple	£49.35
Two children (£10.40 each)	£20.80
Heating addition for child under five	£ 2.20
Total requirements other than housing	£72.35

Your resources are:

Unemployment benefit	£31.45
Addition for dependent wife	£19.40
Two child benefits at £7.25	£14.50
Total resources	£65.35

Source: *State Benefits: a Guide for Trade Unionists*, Labour Research, LRD Publications, 1987

5.4
Take the kids to McDonald's

In April 1988, for children under the age of eleven, Income Support allowed £1.53 per day to meet all of a child's needs. The price of a Big Mac, Milkshake and French Fries in April 1988 was £2.29.

In carrying out Activities 1 and 2, you will certainly have had difficulty in deciding what is 'necessary' and what is 'desirable'. You will have realised that these are matters of judgment, and that they are not fixed for all time, all places, and all people.

ACTIVITY 3

(a) Items of expenditure may be classed as NECESSARY, or as DESIRABLE, or as a LUXURY. Make a list of ten items, five household and five personal, under each heading, as they apply to you, personally, in Britain today.

NECESSARY DESIRABLE LUXURY

Household
1.
2.
3.
4.
5.

Personal
1.
2.
3.
4.
5.

(b) Now, using the same items as far as possible, make another set of lists as they might have been in 1940. How are the new lists different?

(c) Now, imagine it is the year 2010. What changes might there be in your lists?

(d) Many other factors would affect these lists. How would they vary according to your age, where you live (region, or urban/rural), your job (if any), your sex, your health, the type of housing you have, the time of year? Are there any other relevant factors?

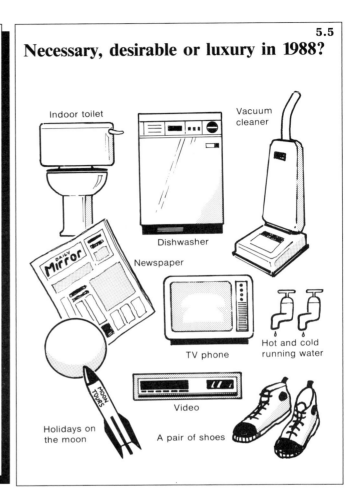

5.5

Necessary, desirable or luxury in 1988?

Indoor toilet

Vacuum cleaner

Dishwasher

Newspaper

TV phone

Hot and cold running water

Video

Holidays on the moon

A pair of shoes

The above activities demonstrate that what counts as **necessary** is relative, rather than absolute. This difficulty has been recognised by sociologists for many years, and has resulted in new ways of defining poverty.

ACTIVITY 4

You will notice a number of similarities between these quotations (5.6).

(a) Study the quotations systematically, and make a list of any ideas or concepts which appear at least once. Make a special note of any that occur more than once.

(b) Using your list from (a), and in not more than about thirty words, complete this sentence:
'Relative poverty is . . . . . .'

(c) Again in not more than thirty words, complete this sentence:
'Absolute poverty is . . . . . .'

5.6

(a) Poverty is a word that is used in at least three different ways. Each poses questions which every society should be prepared to answer. The first usage poses questions about hardship, misery and 'destitution poverty'. . . conditons which are still occasionally to be found among low-paid workers as well as people out of work. The second usage poses questions about the incomes, wealth and real living standards of different kinds of people: the answers will not provide a scientific measure of 'subsistence poverty', for that cannot be clearly defined, but they will show whose living standards are lowest and may suggest the reasons for these patterns. The third usage poses questions about inequality, exclusion, discrimination, injustice and 'relative poverty'. . . I believe that poverty means a standard of living so low that it excludes people from the community in which they live.
Source: Donnison, D. *The Politics of Poverty*, Martin Robertson, London, 1982

(b) To keep out of poverty. . . people must have an income which enables them to participate in the life of the community. They must be able, for example, to keep themselves reasonably fed, and well enough dressed to maintain their self-respect and to attend interviews for jobs with confidence. Their homes must be reasonably warm; their children should not feel shamed by the quality of their clothing; the family must be able to visit relatives, and give them something on their birthdays and at Christmas time; they must be able to read newspapers, and retain their television sets and their membership of trade unions and churches. And they must be able to live in a way which ensures, so far as possible, that public officials, doctors, teachers, landlords and others must treat them with the courtesy due to every member of the community.
Source: Donnison, *op. cit.*

(c) Individuals, families and groups in the population can be said to be in poverty when they lack the resources to obtain the types of diet, participate in the activities and have the living conditions and amenities which are customary, or are at least widely encouraged or approved, in the societies to which they belong. Their resources are so seriously below those commanded by the average individual or family that they are, in effect, excluded from ordinary living patterns, customs and activities.
Source: Townsend, P. *Poverty in the United Kingdom*, Penguin, Harmondsworth, 1979

(d) People are poverty-stricken when their income, even if adequate for survival, falls markedly behind that of the community. Then they cannot have what the larger community regards as the minimum necessary for decency.
Source: Galbraith, J. K. *The Affluent Society*, Penguin, Harmondsworth, 1970

(e) To have one bowl of rice in a society where all other people have half a bowl may well be a sign of achievement and intelligence . . . To have five bowls of rice in a society where the majority have a decent, balanced diet is a tragedy.
Source: Harrington, M. *The Other America*, Macmillan, London, 1962

(f) Poverty is not only about shortage of money. It is about rights and relationships; about how people are treated and how they regard themselves; about powerlessness, exclusion and loss of dignity.
Source: Church House, *Faith in the City*, 1985

(g) Poor people in Britain are not, of course, as poor as those in the Third World. But their poverty is real enough nonetheless. For poverty is a relative, as well as an absolute concept. It exists, even in a relatively rich western society, if people are denied access to what is generally regarded as a reasonable standard and quality of life in that city.
Source: Church House, *op. cit.*

(h) Persons beset by poverty: individuals or families whose resources are so small as to exclude them from the minimum acceptable way of life of the Member State in which they live.

Source: EEC, *Final report of the first programme of pilot schemes and studies to combat poverty*, Commission of the European Communities, 1981

ACTIVITY 5

Using your definitions of absolute and relative poverty from Activity 4, consider the situations of the people in the pictures. Are they poor? If so, in what sense, absolute or relative? Give reasons for your answers.

5.7

Ethiopia

5.8

A flat in Gateshead

Measuring poverty

Most contemporary sociologists adopt a relative definition of poverty. But such a definition still has to be 'operationalised', that is put into a form that can be measured. In our society the obvious way to do this is in terms of money.

Some writers use the Supplementary Benefit scales as a poverty line, saying that any individual or family whose income falls below these levels is in poverty. Many studies, including some done by the DHSS, have taken 140% of SB rates as a poverty line. The Child Poverty Action Group calls this being 'on the margins of poverty'.

ACTIVITY 6

(a) Data 5.9 shows increases in the extent of poverty from 1979–1983. Using the data, explain in a sentence the effect of changing the definition of the poverty line.

(b) 'Lines have to be drawn where none may be visible and they have to be made bold. Where one draws the line is itself a battlefield.' (M. Desai, 1986)

Comment on this using data 5.9.

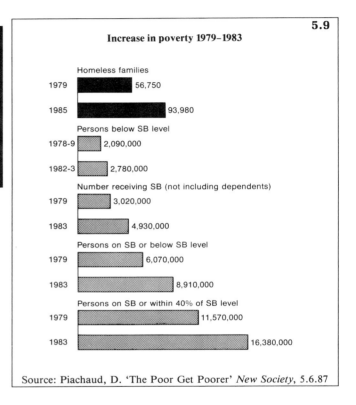

5.9

Increase in poverty 1979–1983

Homeless families
1979 56,750
1985 93,980

Persons below SB level
1978-9 2,090,000
1982-3 2,780,000

Number receiving SB (not including dependents)
1979 3,020,000
1983 4,930,000

Persons on SB or below SB level
1979 6,070,000
1983 8,910,000

Persons on SB or within 40% of SB level
1979 11,570,000
1983 16,380,000

Source: Piachaud, D. 'The Poor Get Poorer' *New Society*, 5.6.87

In 1979, Professor Peter Townsend's major study *Poverty in the United Kingdom* was published. Using the concept of **relative deprivation**, he attempted 'to define the style of living which is generally shared or approved in each society, and find whether there is ... a point in the scale of the distribution of resources below which, as resources diminish, families find it particularly difficult to share in the customs, activitities and diets comprising their society's style of living.' He compiled a 'deprivation index' to cover 'major aspects of dietary, household, familial, recreational and social deprivation'.

ACTIVITY 7

Apply this index to yourself.

(a) How many of the items apply to you or to your household? How many of them would have to apply before you felt able to say, 'That makes me poor'?

(b) Why do you not have the items you have identified yourself as lacking? Is it always because of a lack of money?

(c) Note any items on the 'deprivation index' which you think should not be there. Give reasons for your answers.

Townsend's deprivation index 5.10

1. Has not had a week's holiday away from home in last twelve months.
2. (Adults) Has not had a relative or friend to the home for a meal or snack in the last four weeks.
3. (Adults) Has not been out in the last four weeks to a relative or friend for a meal or snack.
4. (Children under fifteen) Has not had a friend to play or to tea in the last four weeks.
5. (Children) Did not have a party on last birthday.
6. Has not had an afternoon or evening out for entertainment in the last two weeks.
7. Does not have fresh meat (including meals out) as many as four days a week.
8. Has gone through one or more days in the past fortnight without a cooked meal.
9. Has not had a cooked breakfast most days of the week.
10. Household does not have a refrigerator.
11. Household does not usually have a Sunday joint.
12. Household does not have sole use of four amenities indoors (flush WC; sink or washbasin and cold-water tap; fixed bath or shower; and gas or electric cooker).

Source: Townsend *op. cit.*

Using this index, Townsend showed that, the lower people's incomes, the greater their deprivation. He also found that there was a level of income below which the rate of increase of deprivation accelerated. This point was at about 150% of SB levels. 'As income diminishes from the highest levels, so deprivation steadily increases, but below 150% of the supplementary benefit standard, deprivation begins to increase swiftly.' This he called 'The Deprivation Standard' of poverty.

But Townsend has his critics as data 5.12 shows.

ACTIVITY 8
Write a short statement showing where Townsend and Piachaud are in agreement, and where they disagree.

5.13

'I'm the chairman of a multinational, a vegetarian, I have Weetabix for breakfast, I have no time for relatives and friends or entertainment. I am very rich happy and successful. My only problem – I don't do very well on the deprivation index.'

5.12

Piachaud vs. Townsend

The first problem arises with the components of Townsend's deprivation index. It is not clear what some of them have to do with poverty, nor how some of them were selected. Some of the components may certainly have a direct link with poverty... the holiday, the evening's entertainments, the refrigerator and the household amenities, but other components... fresh meat, cooked meals, cooked breakfast and Sunday joint... may be as much to do with tastes as with poverty.

Townsend's index offers no solution to the intractable problem of disentangling the effects of differences in tastes from those of differences in income...

What surely matters most is the choice a person has, and the constraints he or she faces. To choose not to go on holiday or eat meat is one thing: it may interest sociologists, but it is of no interest to those concerned with poverty. To have little or no opportunity to take a holiday or buy meat is entirely different.

The most strange and unsatisfactory feature in Townsend's conception of relative deprivation is its emphasis on styles of living. His deprivation index concerns itself with a number of primarily private aspects of behaviour. He does not include in his index more social aspects, such as deprivation at work, of environment, or of public services. He does discuss these extensively elsewhere in his study...

This is not to question that poverty is a relative concept, or that there is real poverty in the United Kingdom. Nor is it to accept that the state's poverty standard, the supplementary benefit standard, is adequate... But Townsend has not substantiated his claim of scientific objectivity.

Source: Piachaud, D. 'Peter Townsend and the Holy Grail' *New Society*, 10.9.81

Sociologists have shifted the emphasis of their definitions of poverty away from the basic necessities to sustain life, and towards what is necessary for a satisfactory standard of living and to achieve participation in everyday social life.

But what are the customary standards of living in our society? How can they be ascertained? Who is to say what they are?

Mack and Lansley (1985) argued that the best way to find out what are considered to be the necessities of life in our society is to ask people. Their 'Breadline Britain' survey aimed to identify 'the minimum acceptable way of life for Britain in the 1980s'. Those who have no choice but to fall below this minimum level can be said to be "in poverty"...this means that the "necessities" of life are identified by public opinion and not by, on the one hand, the views of experts or, on the other hand, the norms of behaviour per se.'

Mack and Lansley made a list of things which relate to people's standard of living, and then asked a sample of just under twelve hundred people which items they thought were necessities in Britain in 1983, which were desirable, and which they were unsure about.

From the responses they obtained, Mack and Lansley operationalised their concept of a 'consensual view of need'. They identified as necessities the items which the highest percentage of people identified as essential.

In the second part of their survey, they asked people which items they did not themselves have, and whether this was because they didn't want them or because they couldn't afford them. They took 'all those who cannot afford three or more necessities as an indication of the numbers in poverty'. This definition, then, is not made in terms of cash income, though those who could not afford three or more necessities were heavily concentrated among those on the lowest incomes.

ACTIVITY 9
List the advantages and disadvantages of the 'Breadline Britain' measurement of poverty.

5.14
The public's perception of necessities

Standard-of-living items in rank order	% classing items as necessity	Standard-of-living items in rank order	% classing items as necessity
1. Heating to warm living areas of the home if it's cold	97	19. A hobby or leisure activity	64
2. Indoor toilet (not shared with another household)	96	20. Two hot meals a day (for adults)	64
3. Damp-free home	96	21. Meat or fish every other day	63
4. Bath (not shared with another household)	94	22. Presents for friends or family once a year	63
5. Beds for everyone in the household	94	23. A holiday away from home for one week a year, not with relatives	63
6. Public transport for one's needs	88	24. Leisure equipment for children e.g. sports equipment or a bicycle[a]	57
7. A warm water-proof coat	87	25. A garden	55
8. Three meals a day for children[a]	82	26. A television	51
9. Self-contained accomodation	79	27. A 'best outfit' for special occasions	48
10. Two pairs of all-weather shoes	78	28. A telephone	43
11. Enough bedrooms for every child over 10 of different sex to have his/her own[a]	77	29. An outing for children once a week[a]	40
12. Refrigerator	77	30. A dressing gown	38
13. Toys for children[a]	71	31. Children's friends round for tea/a snack once a fortnight[a]	37
14. Carpets in living rooms and bedrooms	70	32. A night out once a fortnight (adults)	36
15. Celebrations on special occasions such as Christmas	69	33. Friends/family round for a meal once a month	32
16. A roast meat joint or its equivalent once a week	67	32. A car	22
17. A washing-machine	67	35. A packet of cigarettes every other day	14
18. New, not second-hand clothes	64		

Average of all 35 items = 64.1

[a]For families with children only.

Source: Mack J. and Lansley S. *Poor Britain* Allen & Unwin, London, 1985

By now, it will be very clear to you that the 'poverty line' is fixed at different levels by different people. In an article in *New Society* in 1984, Paul Ashton identified five well-known definitions of poverty (though he argues that some of them are more to do with deprivation than with poverty) and calculated the numbers in poverty according to each definition.

ACTIVITY 10
(a) Imagine that the government of the day has just published the latest figures about the number of people receiving Supplementary Benefit. Imagine too that you are an opponent of the government. Using data 5.15 write a letter to a newspaper in which you argue that SB figures understate the problem of poverty.

(b) Now write a reply to this letter, in which you argue that the problem of poverty in this country has been largely solved.

5.15
Numbers in poverty (millions)

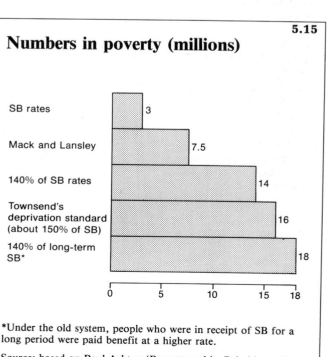

SB rates	3
Mack and Lansley	7.5
140% of SB rates	14
Townsend's deprivation standard (about 150% of SB)	16
140% of long-term SB*	18

*Under the old system, people who were in receipt of SB for a long period were paid benefit at a higher rate.

Source: based on Paul Ashton 'Poverty and its Beholders', *New Society*, 18.10.84

Drawing the poverty line is not just a matter of social scientists disagreeing, because the numbers of people who are in poverty is an important political issue. Both Townsend and his critics recognise the political aspects of the debate. Data 5.16 provides a right-wing response to Townsend's left-wing views.

ACTIVITY 11

(a) According to Peregrine Worsthorne (5.16), 'the best way of helping the poor is to create more wealth'.

What would be the effect on the numbers defined as being in poverty if everybody's standard of living went up by a proportionately equal amount taking
 (i) an absolute definition of poverty,
 (ii) a relative definition of poverty?

Which definition does Worsthorne seem to favour?

(b) Define the following terms as they are used by Worsthorne.
 (i) poverty;
 (ii inequality;
 (iii) relative deprivation.

(c) Do you agree with Worsthorne's argument? Briefly state your reasons.

5.17

ACCORDING TO OUR MAGGIE "SOCIAL DILAPIDATIONS CAN BE ATTENDED TO ONLY AFTER SOME RENAISSANCE IN THE PRODUCTIVE SYSTEM"...... HENCE THE CUTS... OR IN PLAIN ENGLISH.....

YOU GET POORER WHILE WE GET RICHER. BUT DONT DESPAIR 'COS WHEN WE'RE REALLY STINKING RICH WE'LL THINK ABOUT THINKING ABOUT YOU.

BRICK

5.16

Poverty or inequality?

Townsend's extremely voluminous *Poverty in the United Kingdom* contends that about one quarter of the British population lives in a state of actual or near poverty...For this dire state of affairs Professor Townsend, of course, blames capitalism or 'the principles of allocation of resources and social sponsorship'...

But nowhere does it seem to occur to Professor Townsend that the best way of helping the poor is to create more wealth. Like many men of the left, he apparently conceives of the national economy as a cake which cannot grow any bigger. All you can do is to cut it up in different ways. This is economic nonsense, and such a redistribution would be of no material benefit whatsoever to the poor whom ...presumably...Professor Townsend wants to help.

Much of what the professor describes as poverty does not deserve that dread word at all.

In his view poverty means relative deprivation. Thus anyone whose income falls below the average runs the risk of being described as poverty-stricken...If that is how Professor Townsend wishes to use the term he is obviously at liberty to do so. But where I take issue with him is in his assumption that poverty so described should provoke moral outrage. To my way of thinking, poverty can be morally outrageous only if the condition contravenes some absolute yardstick as to what is morally acceptable...Compared with most human beings alive in the world today, Professor Townsend's victims are rich beyond the dreams of avarice. They are only poor in relation to contemporary British standards of affluence. Their condition is only shocking because it is not as comfortable as that of those who are better off. What is offensive to Professor Townsend, in short, is not so much the existence of poverty in Britain as the existence of inequality...To pretend that one is interested in curing poverty, when one is really concerned about rectifying inequality, is intellectually dishonest, since it is to exploit feelings that are common to everybody for a purpose that is highly partisan...Short of imposing a uniform standard of living, there is no way of eradicating relative deprivation...However much the lot of the poor is improved, there will always be a superior standard of living by comparison with which the poor remain under-privileged.

Source: Peregrine Worsthorne in *The Daily Telegraph*, 27.10.79

ACTIVITY 12

(a) What will be the effect on the official statistics of the numbers of people living below SB level if the SB rates are raised?

(b) Between 1978 and 1987 SB rose by about 5% in real terms (that is, after allowing for inflation).
Write a paragraph for the election manifesto of the government which presided over this increase, and is now seeking re-election.

(c) Over the same period, real disposable income (how much money people actually had to spend) rose by 14% in real terms.
Write a paragraph for the election manifesto of the party which was in Opposition during this period, and which is now seeking election to become the government.

5.18

Conclusion

This unit opened with these two apparently contradictory statements.

'Want in the sense of absolute deprivation, has been largely eliminated.'
(Green Paper on Social Security Reform 1985)
'The past five years have witnesssed a high-water mark in the rising tide of poverty.'
(Pond and Burghes, 1986)

Looking at them again, now you should be able to see that the contradiction arises from the fact that the two statements are based on different definitions of poverty, absolute and relative.

And when it is pointed out that the first quotation comes from a government source, and the second from an article co-authored by the Director of the Low Pay Unit, one of the anti-poverty pressure groups, it will also be clear that the definition and measurement of poverty is not a neutral activity. In fact, the debate about the causes, extent and consequences of poverty is one of the most critical in contemporary politics.

Further reading

Child Poverty Action Group *Poverty: the Facts*, CPAG, London, 1987 [useful list of CAPG publications available from 1–5 Bath Street, London, EC1V 9PX]
Harrison, P. *Inside the Inner City*, Penguin, Harmondsworth, 1983
Mack, J., Lansley, S. *Poor Britain*, George Allen & Unwin, London, 1985
Townsend, P. *Poverty in the United Kingdom*, Penguin, Harmondsworth, 1979 [especially first two chapters; a long book – read selectively]
New Statesman and Society – frequent items on poverty and welfare

UNIT 6   Unemployment

The aim of this unit is to help you explore some of the major issues and debates surrounding unemployment – its measurement and distribution, its effects on the individual and society, its causes and solutions and prospects for the future.

Introduction

Unemployment is *the* economic, political and social issue of our times. It is the basis of the growing divisions in British society between rich and poor, North and South, Conservative and Labour, employed and unemployed. It has lain behind the major social conflicts of the 1980s – the Inner City Riots, the 1984 Miners' Strike, the 1985 Printers' Dispute. It has helped generate the growth of such modern social diseases as crime, poverty, ill-health and divorce. It is at the heart of any contemporary discussion about social order and social conflict, social change and stratification. It affects – possibly infects – every major social institution from democracy to the Rule of Law. It threatens every family, every community, every institution.

Unemployment – the 'official' facts

ACTIVITY 1

Charts 6.1, 6.2 and 6.3 are compiled from official statistics. Using the following questions as a guide, analyse this official picture of unemployment:

(a) What was the official figure for unemployment in 1987?

(b) In which year did unemployment rise the most?

(c) Does chart 6.1 confirm or refute the present government's claim that the underlying trend in unemployment is now down? What is an underlying trend?

(d) Which categories of people in terms of age, occupation and region have suffered the worst unemployment and why? (charts 6.2 and 6.3)

(e) Which government department deals with unemployment?

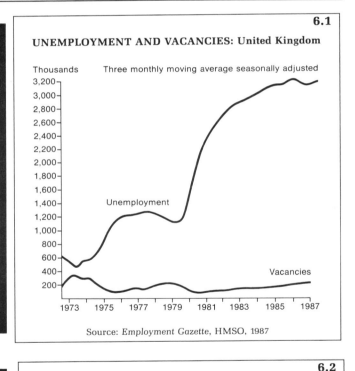

6.1

UNEMPLOYMENT AND VACANCIES: United Kingdom

Thousands   Three monthly moving average seasonally adjusted

Source: *Employment Gazette*, HMSO, 1987

ACTIVITY 2

(a) Draw a map of the UK and, using data 6.2, put in each area's unemployment rate

(b) Does the resultant picture support or refute the claim that Britain today is a 'Divided Nation'?

(c) What other evidence of social, political and economic division would you require to support such a thesis fully?

6.2

Unemployment by region

Unemployment	
1.	N. Ireland	20.3%
2.	North	15.3%
3.	Scotland	14.5%
4.	Wales	14.3%
5.	North West	14%
6.	Yorks & Humberside	12.7%
7.	West Midlands	12.1%
8.	East Midlands	9.9%
9.	South West	9.3%
10.	South East	7.7%
11.	East Anglia	7.6%
	United Kingdom	11.1%

Source: *The Daily Telegraph*, 9.6.88

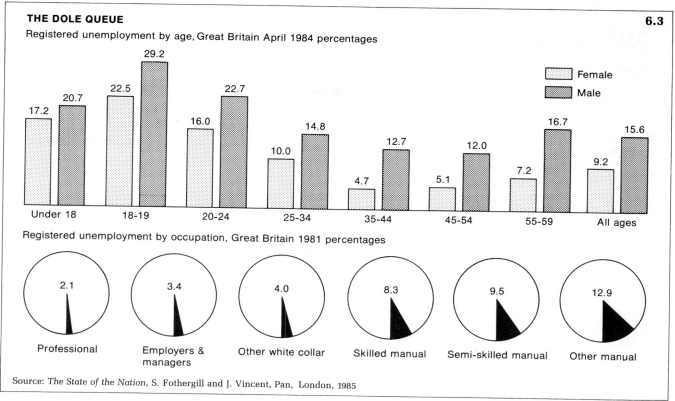

THE DOLE QUEUE 6.3

Registered unemployment by age, Great Britain April 1984 percentages

Registered unemployment by occupation, Great Britain 1981 percentages

Source: *The State of the Nation*, S. Fothergill and J. Vincent, Pan, London, 1985

Unemployment – the 'unofficial' statistics

The official unemployment statistics, however, have been extensively criticised, with some critics even going so far as to accuse the present Government of 'fiddling the figures' as a way of making unemployment disappear. The T.U.C. and Labour Party, for example, have put the true total for unemployment at 4 million or more. In contrast, right wing organisations like the Aims of Industry have put the number of 'genuinely unemployed' nearer the one million mark. David Lipsey sums up the statistical debate in data 6.4

ACTIVITY 3

(a) Re-draw table 6.4 listing only those categories of unemployed you would include.

(b) What is *your* estimate of the real total of unemployment?

(c) Explain why you included certain groups and excluded others.

6.4

Unemployment – the statistical debate

To government figures of 3,094,000 unemployed

Left-wing critics ADD:		Right-wing critics SUBTRACT:	
Unemployed excluded by statistical changes, October 1982 (net)	189,000	School leavers	168,000
		Claimants who are not really looking for jobs[1]	490,000
Unemployed over-sixties (no longer required to register)[1]	199,000	Severely disabled	23,000
Short-time working	43,000	"Unemployables" – mentally or physically incapable[2]	135,000
Students on vacation	27,000	"Job changers" – out of work for four weeks or less	360,000
Effects of Special Employment Measures	395,000		
Unregistered unemployed[2]	490,000	"Black economy" workers, illegally claiming benefit[3]	250,000
Total additions	1,343,000	Total subtractions	1,426,000
TOTAL UNEMPLOYED	4,437,000	TOTAL UNEMPLOYED	1,668,000

1. Of whom 37,000 were removed between Dec 1981 and February 1982 and a further 162,000 as a result of Budget 1983 measures.
2. Estimate based on Dept of Employment survey, 1981.

1. Estimate, based on 1981 Labour Force Survey.
2. Dept. of Employment estimate.
3. Unknowable: estimate based on internal government survey suggesting 8% of claims not justified

Source: David Lipsey in *The Sunday Times*, 6.11.83

John Prescott, Labour employment spokesman, and other critics of the present Conservative Government have claimed that it has 'fiddled' the unemployment figures by:-

- excluding legitimate categories of unemployed;
- pushing people off the dole queue into schemes such as the Y.T.S.

ACTIVITY 4

(a) How far do tables 6.5 and 6.6 support these critics' claims?

(b) How far do tables 6.5 and 6.6 support the Government's view:
- that such exclusions make the official statistics more accurate?
- that such categories of people *should* be excluded from the unemployment statistics?

(c) Explain the term 'seasonally adjusted'.

(d) Why, in table 6.5, does the 'Inclusion of self-employed and H.M. Forces in the denominator of the unemployed percentage' lead to a 1.4% fall in the unemployment rate?

(e) From your point of view, make brief comments on data 6.7, 6.8 and 6.9

6.5

CHANGES IN THE UNEMPLOYMENT STATISTICS

Date	Change	Effect
10/79	Fortnightly payment of benefits.	+20,000
11/81	Men over 60 offered higher supplementary benefit to leave working population.	−37,000
10/82	Registration at job centres made voluntary. Computer count of benefit claimants substituted for clerical count of registrants.	−190,000
3/83	Men 60 and over given national insurance credits or higher supplementary benefit without claiming unemployment benefit.	−162,000
7/85	Correction of Northern Ireland discrepancies.	−5,000
3/86	Two-week delay in compilation of figures to reduce over-recording.	−50,000
		424,000

Total effect of changes to seasonally adjusted figure without school leavers in 4/87.   458,000

| 7/86 | Inclusion of self-employed and HM forces in denominator of unemployed percentage. | −1.4% |

Sources: *Employment Gazette*, October 1986, p. 422. *Unemployment Bulletin*, no. 20, summer 1986, pp. 14-15, and statistical supplement, May 1986, p. 6.

Source: *Lloyds Bank Economic Bulletin*, Sept. 1987

6.6

SPECIAL EMPLOYMENT MEASURES

	Thousands off unemployment count March 1987
1. Job creation programmes	
Community programme	220
New workers' scheme	6
Enterprise allowance scheme	15
2. Administrative/statistical measures	
Job release scheme	23
Availability for work test	6
Restart scheme	104
Benefit changes	15
3. Training schemes	
Job training scheme	0[1]
Youth training scheme	0[1]
	389

1. Numbers are difficult to estimate, and thought to be negligible.

Source: *Lloyds Bank Economic Bulletin*, Sept. 1987

6.7

There are lies, damned lies and unemployment statistics

6.8

6.9

Mr John Prescott, Labour's employment spokesman, said that "eight years of cynical manipulation of the unemployment figures have at last produced the Government's election target of registered unemployment below three million".

Source: *The Guardian*, 19.6.87

The jobs gap

Unemployment statistics, however, are only one side of the unemployment equation. What is also important is:
● the number of job vacancies;
● the demand for jobs – this depends heavily on the age and sex structure of the labour force.

Chart 6.10 shows the present 'Jobs Gap'. Table 6.11 shows how job vacancies have risen and fallen in the period 1979–1987.

ACTIVITY 5

(a) How wide is the present 'jobs gap'? (chart 6.10)

(b) In which area of employment (table 6.11) has there been:
 – the greatest decline?
 – the greatest increase?

(c) Explain the following terms:
 – working population
 – employed labour force.

(d) Explain why the demand for jobs depends heavily on the age and sex structure of the labour force.

(e) The statistics on 'job vacancies' and on the 'self-employed' are usually considered to be unreliable. Why?

(f) The present Government has claimed that:-
'Since we were re-elected in 1983, the number of jobs in Britain has grown by one million.'
 (i) How true is this statement acording to table 6.11?
 (ii) Critics claim that not all those jobs are REAL jobs. What do you think a 'real' job is?
 (iii) Why hasn't this one million increase in jobs led to a one million decrease in unemployment?

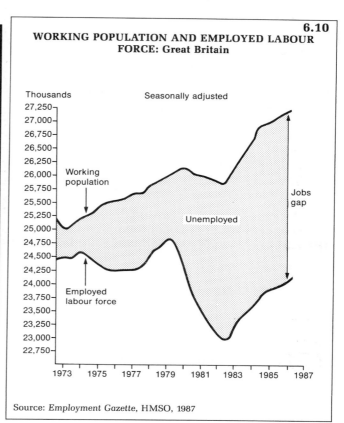

6.10

WORKING POPULATION AND EMPLOYED LABOUR FORCE: Great Britain

Source: *Employment Gazette*, HMSO, 1987

6.11

CHANGES IN EMPLOYMENT AND UNEMPLOYMENT 1979-87
Great Britain, seasonally adjusted

	March 1979 000's	March 1983 000's	March 1987 000's
1. Manufacturing employees	7129	5485	5075
2. Other employees	15413	15044	16182
3. All employees	22542	20529	21257
4. Self-employed	1843	2147	2644
5. HM Forces	314	322	320
6. Employed labour force	24699	22998	24221
7. Unemployed	1199	2828	3116
8. Working population	25898	25826	27337
9. Inactive population	6672	7474	6730
10. Working age population	32570	33300	34067
Activity rate = 8/10	79.5%	77.5%	80.2%

Source: *Lloyds Bank Economic Bulletin*, No. 105, Sept. 1987

The effects of unemployment

The social, economic and political effects of mass unemployment are enormous – but difficult to measure! Consider *first* the impact on the INDIVIDUAL.

ACTIVITY 6

(a) Explain how unemployment may cause:
   – stress
   – ill-health and early death
   – poverty.

(b) According to Dr. Smith (6.13),
   (i) How many people are likely to die prematurely before the turn of the century because of unemployment?
   (ii) What are the other possible effects of unemployment?

(c) Why does Dr. Smith think these figures may be an underestimate?

(d) Does unemployment affect women in the same way as men? If not, why not?

(e) Try to criticise the above thesis that unemployment 'causes' social ills such as crime, divorce and suicide.

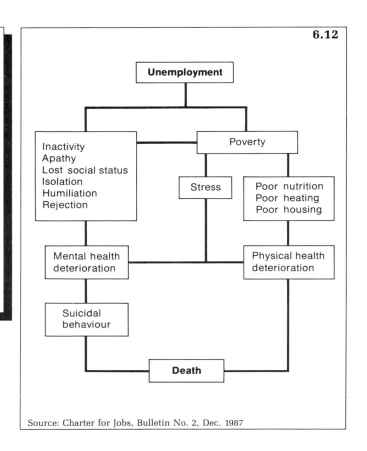

6.12

Source: Charter for Jobs, Bulletin No. 2, Dec. 1987

6.13

Unemployment blamed for 3,000 deaths a year

**By Andrew Veitch,
Medical Correspondent**

Unemployment is killing at least 3,000 people a year, according to an analysis published yesterday.

"Forty thousand are going to die prematurely before the turn of the century unless we do something dramatic about unemployment," says Dr Richard Smith, assistant editor of the British Medical Journal.

Unemployed men were more than twice as likely to commit suicide than the rest of the population. They were 40 per cent more likely to die of cancer, and 75 per cent more likely to die of lung cancer.

Surveys had shown that unemployed men were more likely to need medical help and to be referred to hospitals for treatment.

Mr Smith said the figures were likely to be an underestimate, because they did not include deaths among women out of work, deaths among children in unemployed families, men who registered as chronically sick even though their real problem was that they could not find work, or those who had retired early.

Babies born to unemployed parents tended to be smaller, and thus less likely to survive. Poor nutrition and poor housing as a result of poverty were probably to blame.

Stress was probably an important cause of

illness among unemployed men, according to Dr Smith's analysis. Social isolation, and the loss of a sense of purpose and self-worth played a part. The "corrosive" effects of poverty probably did much of the rest of the damage.

"Most unemployed people who have tried time and again to get a job have been endlessly humiliated and beaten down," Dr Smith said.

Edinburgh studies had shown that unemployment was causing young people to turn to drugs.

'Unemployment and Health', by Dr Richard Smith, Oxford University Press.

Secondly, consider the impact of unemployment on the SOCIAL STRUCTURE OF SOCIETY.

ACTIVITY 7

(a) What does Paul Harrison mean by the phrase 'a welfare state in reverse'?

(b) How far does the evidence in table 6.15 support Paul Harrison's claim that 'unemployment has become a vast engine for increasing the existing inequalities in British society'?

(c) What other factors beside occupation need to be taken into account in analysing INEQUALITY?

6.14

Unemployment became a vast engine for increasing the existing inequalities in British society – a welfare state in reverse gear. There was no question of equality of sacrifice in the fight against inflation. The belts of those who were thinnest had to be tightened hardest. The most disadvantaged areas and the most disadvantaged people were hit most brutally. The Hackney figures tell a sad tale, paralleling national developments. Unemployment hit manual workers harder than non-manual: between 1979 and 1980, 14 per cent of jobs in the 'operative' category disappeared, but less than half of one per cent of office jobs. It hit women harder than men; between 1979 and 1981, female unemployment rose at twice the rate of male. Black unemployment rose twice as fast as white. Recession hit the young harder than the old, the unskilled harder than the skilled, the disabled harder than the fit. Equally germane to our tale, unemployment hit disadvantaged areas harder than the advantaged, the already lagging Celtic and northern peripheries and the inner cities suffering by far the worst.

Source: *Inside the Inner City*, Paul Harrison, Penguin, Harmondsworth, 1985

6.15

Those without a job and actively seeking work as a proportion of those economically active (Great Britain)

previous social class	spring 1979	spring 1985	change
		percentage	
1 professional etc.	*	1.5	*
2 intermediate	1.6	3.5	+1.9
3 skilled	3.0	6.7	+3.7
4 partly skilled	5.2	9.6	+4.4
5 unskilled	8.2	12.7	+4.5
all unemployed	5.6	10.6	+5.0

The 1980s have seen a series of violent upheavals. Inner city riots exploded in 1981 and 1985. The miners' strike 1984/85 was marked by violent encounters between strikers and police as was the Wapping dispute of 1985–1987, a long running confrontation between sacked printers and Rupert Murdoch's News International.

ACTIVITY 8

(a) How far do you think unemployment 'caused' each of these events?

   What other possible 'causes' might have been at work?

(b) To what extent were each of these events 'political'? What is meant by the term 'political'?

6.16

Pickets attempt to break through police lines, Bilston Glen Pit, Edinburgh, 1984

6.17

St. Paul's riots, 1980

6.18

Wapping demonstration, 1987

ACTIVITY 9

Using your own ideas and data 6.19–6.21, try to explain why, with three million unemployed, Britain has NOT had the revolution so many people once predicted.

6.19

We have witnessed no riots of the unemployed. There is no national organisation of the jobless. Crime, drug addiction, suicide, family breakdown and other social evils have grown, in part because of unemployment, but they have failed to make much political impression.

Why is this? A major part of the explanation lies in the characteristics of today's unemployed. They are not a static or homongeneous mass, a disciplined and self-conscious reserve army on the margins of the labour market, simply waiting to be mobilised by politicians. They constitute a constantly shifting, variegated collection of people, more than one in three of whom have not had a full-time legitimate job for over a year.

Robert Taylor in *The Observer*, 25.8.85

6.20

Supplementary Benefit Office, Bloomsbury, London

We are an army here. The battles we fight are for giros that fail to arrive, for money which, when it does come, we cannot possibly live on. This is our battleground, this place, and if proof is needed just look at these glass cages, at the wire mesh barriers, at the bars on the windows – the display of an occupying force.

Source: Ben Morris, 'A Doleful Existence', *New Society*, 7.8.87

6.21

LAMPPOSTS ON STREET CORNERS SHOW 'LEANING SYNDROME'

ACTIVITY 10

Mrs. Thatcher has always argued that THERE IS NO ALTERNATIVE (TINA) to her policies, that unemployment is not as serious a problem as inflation and that post-war governments were wrong to use so much public money trying to create jobs and keep 'lame duck' industries going.

(a) How far do you think she was right?

(b) Radical critics of this government have used the concept of HEGEMONY proposed by the Italian Marxist Antonion Gramsci to argue that Mrs. Thatcher has established ideological domination over Britain in the 1980s.

   (i) What is meant by the term HEGEMONY? (data 6.22)

   (ii) What evidence is there to support this point of view?

   (iii) How might the media and education systems help create a particular ideological climate of opinion? Give examples of such ideological conditioning.

   (iv) Critically evaluate this thesis.

6.22

Hegemony

The term HEGEMONY is commonly used to indicate a state of consensual predominance of the powerful group or class in a society or social system over the ruled. It covers the whole range of norms and values, not just the political, involved in the ruling group's view of the world. A ruling class or group to which legitimacy is given has achieved hegemony; its rule is accepted without question and alternatives are not mooted. A hegemonic class imposes its own views on society as a whole.

Source: *Macmillan Encyclopaedia of Sociology*

Such IDEOLOGICAL dominance in a capitalist society is achieved through the Ruling Class's control of such powerful institutions as the media and education systems.

Causes and solutions

'The only sovereign remedy yet discovered by democracies for unemployment is total war.'
William H. Beveridge, 1944

Causes – It is impossible in the space available to review all the possible causes of unemployment, but table 6.24 lists some of the most strongly argued.

ACTIVITY 11

(a) Select *three* of the causes you consider most important and explain them in detail.

(b) Suggest one other cause not included in the table.

(c) Re-draw table 6.24 listing the causes most likely to be cited by Conservative politicians on the right and by Labour politicians on the left.

(d) Explain why Conservative views as to the causes of unemployment tend to be so different from those of left-wingers.

6.24

- Inflation
- Government Policy
- Poor Management
- Bureaucracy
- Married Women returning to work
- Immigration
- Social Security Benefits too high
- Trade Unions
- New Technology
- World Economy
- Lack of Investment
- Lack of Skills

6.23

STOP/GO

BOX 5

EMPLOYMENT OFF

BZZZZZZZZZZ

BUDOYNNK!

'MICROELECTRONIC DEVICES WILL NOT CREATE MORE JOBS'

Solutions – The following solutions to mass unemployment were offered by the three major political parties in their 1987 manifestos.

ACTIVITY 12

(a) Explain in your *own* words the three solutions offered.

(b) What are the main differences in the three proposals? Why are they so different?

(c) Which 'solution' would you have chosen and why?

(d) Two of the parties proposed dramatic increases in government spending. What might be the ill-effects of such expenditure?

(e) Why did the Conservative Party propose increasing tax disincentives against women?

(f) How has the Conservative Government tackled unemployment over the past eight years?
In what ways have its policies differed from previous post-war governments?

6.25

CONSERVATIVE	LABOUR	LIBERAL – SDP
New Job training schemes for 18–25 year-olds to build on YTS and other re-skilling measures (and help reduce jobless figures). Discouragement of annual pay round, national pay settlements and comparabilities. Emphasis on performance related pay. Tax disincentives against women workers increased.	Six billion pounds a year job package aimed at creating 1.2 million new jobs and reducing unemployment by one million in two years. Half the new jobs in construction and new skills training. The rest in private manufacturing and local authority enterprise. Annual economic assessment to include discussion of pay. National minimum wage.	Unemployment cut to two million by 1989 in 1.6 billion pound jobs package. Job guarantees to long-term unemployed. Priority drive against skills shortages. Training tax on employers. Education and training grants to 16–19 year-olds. Regional industrial development. Boost for small firms. Expansion of voluntary sector.

Academic perspectives on unemployment

Academic perspectives on unemployment are equally divided as to the causes and solutions to unemployment. Below are two very different 'perspectives' on unemployment, one by Professor Minford, a strong supporter of Mrs. Thatcher and Monetarism; the other by Roger Simon in a Communist Party booklet, outlining a marxist perspective.

ACTIVITY 13

(a) What are the main differences between these two points of view (6.26 and 6.27) in terms of
   (i) CAUSES of mass unemployment,
   (ii) SOLUTIONS to mass unemployment?

(b) Monetarist writers tend to see mass unemployment as a temporary problem which will be solved once 'market forces' are fully liberated. Marxist writers see unemployment as a form of social control and a reflection of the underlying class struggle in capitalist societies.

   Which do you agree with, and why?

Monetarist solutions to unemployment

6.26

A Monetarist view

The first and most basic cause is the operation of the unemployment benefit system. The minimum flat rate benefit including any supplementary benefit 'top-up' is paid indefinitely to an unemployed man for as long as he remains unemployed; such a man will very naturally expect to be re-employed at a wage after tax and work expenses which is at least as high as this benefit, and probably somewhat higher because he may not wish to 'work for nothing', whatever his personal attitude towards work. His work even at this wage may well be poorly motivated because of his lack of reward, so that productivity also suffers. Hence wages cannot effectively fall below this level for even the most unskilled workers. This level then acts as a floor under the whole wage structure, and working practices accepted at this unskilled level may similarly affect higher levels of the occupational structure. It follows that shifts in economic conditions which would warrant a fall in real wage costs, will have only a limited effect on them and unemployment will result instead. This mechanism, in other words, substantially limits the wage flexibility of the UK economic system.

The second major factor is the power of unions to raise wages relative to non-union wages. Given the way the benefit rate sets a floor below the non-union wage, as unions raise wages for their members, the workers who then lose their jobs cannot all find alternative work in the non-union sector because wages there do not fall sufficiently; the overall effect is increased unemployment.

Source P. Minford, *Unemployment, Cause and Cure*, Blackwell, 1984

6.27

"SELF SACRIFICE IS OUR ONLY SALVATION"
Alan Hardman

A Marxist view

Of course, the most serious aspect of crisis and depression is the repeated occurrence of mass unemployment, when millions of working people lose their livelihood. There tends to be significant unemployment even during relatively prosperous periods of capitalist economic development. But in crises large numbers of workers are suddenly excluded altogether from the productive system.

More than a century ago Marx advanced the hypothesis that capitalism required an *industrial reserve army*, a pool of unemployed or poorly paid and insecure workers who would serve to limit the aspirations of other workers for better conditions, and to allow sudden increases in output and employment. Marx agreed that continuous full employment would erode capital's power over labour and thus undermine profits, accumulation and full employment itself. He suggested that only repeated recessions and technical change linked to massive labour shedding would preserve the reserve army and permit continuing accumulation.

The fact of mass unemployment is the most important evidence supporting the Marxist critique of capitalism. Unemployment is the clearest possible indication that the market and employment relationships, which in capitalist ideology are supposed to serve the needs of people, can and do result in the sacrifice of working people to the practice of private money-making in an economy which escapes from rational social control.

Source: R. Simon, *Introducing Marxism*, CP, London, 1986

Employment, unemployment and the future

Finally, what is the future for the unemployed? Is unemployment going to increase? Where are the jobs of the future going to come from? What will be the meaning of work in a post-industrial society?

Table 6.28 shows the way employment has changed in Britain over the past twenty years.

ACTIVITY 14

(a) Which sectors of the British economy – primary, secondary and tertiary – have declined and which grown in the period 1966–82?

(b) (i) How many jobs were lost or gained in this period?
   (ii) Was there a net loss or a net gain?

(c) Does table 6.28 support or refute the claim that tomorrow's jobs lie in the service sector? Explain your answer in detail. If so, are these jobs also likely to give way to new technology or foreign competition?

(d) Where else might new jobs come from? (Consider self-employment, flexi-working, home working.)

(e) Will any of these sources solve the problem of mass unemployment?

6.28

Total Persons in Employment by Sector 1966–82

	Thousands 1966	Thousands 1982	Percentage change 1966–82
Agriculture, forestry and fishing	464.1	346	– 25.5
Mining and quarrying	574.2	325	– 43.4
Food, drink and tobacco	832.1	605	– 27.3
Coal and petroleum products	524.6	26	– 21.1
Chemical and allied trades		388	
Metal manufacture	622.6	294	– 52.8
Mechanical engineering	2,347.7	129	– 36.4
Instrument engineering			
Electrical engineering			
Shipbuilding and marine engineering	200.1	140	– 30.0
Vehicles	845.2	547	– 35.3
Metal goods	596.0	428	– 28.2
Textiles	757.3	298	– 60.5
Total manufacturing	8,976.4	5,644	– 37.1
Construction	1,636.6	1,011	– 38.2
Gas, water and electricity	422.9	329	– 22.2
Total production industries	11,610.1	7,308	– 37.1
Transports and communications	1,609.3	1,372	– 14.8
Distributive trades	2,925.6	2,653	– 9.3
Insurance, banking, finance and business services	638.8	1,305	+ 104.3
Professional and scientific services	2,512.5	3,650	+ 45.3
Miscellaneous services	2,196.0	2,484	+ 13.1
Public administration and defence	1,344.3	1,497	+ 11.4
Total service industries	11,226.5	12,960	+ 15.4
All industries and services	23,300.	20,614	– 11.5

Source: Department of Employment. *Gazette*

Conclusion

I hope by now you can see how central unemployment is to our understanding of modern industrial society, how starkly it reflects the social problems, divisions and seeds of the future.

By working your way through the exercises set in this unit, you should have a deeper and more critical understanding of this key issue – and of how to study it sociologically. Read John Owen's conclusion below and just start to imagine the problems – economic, social and political – that will erupt beneath the surface of Western society soon unless the issue of mass unemployment is recognised and confronted as *the* issue of our times.

The present unemployment problem

Public concern with mass unemployment is today almost universal, and rightly so. In nearly all Western countries, the official level of unemployment has been rising steadily since the 1960s. Between 1979 and mid-1987, the mean rate of unemployment within the O.E.C.D. (Organisation for Economic Co-operation and Development) will have risen from 5.1 to 8.25%. Following these rises, the total number of *officially* jobless will be almost 31 million (just under 20 million of these in Western Europe); and unemployment rates will have risen in every O.E.C.D. country, except the United States and Finland. For unemployment levels to be reduced to the 1979 level of 19 million persons, some 11,000 net new jobs would have to be created *every day* until 1990.

Source: John Owen, *Social Studies Review*, Jan. 1987

Further reading

Handy, C. *The Future of Work*, Blackwell, Oxford, 1984
Harrison, P. *Inside the Inner City*, Penguin, Harmondsworth, 1983
Merrit, G. *World out of Work*, Collins, London, 1982
Owens, J. 'Politics and Unemployment', *Social Studies Review*, Jan. 1987
Seabrook, J. *Unemployment*, Paladin, St. Albans, 1982
New Society/Society Today, especially 'Unemployment' (30.10.80) and 'The Future of Work' (8 and 15.11.85)

UNIT 7   The Secularization Debate

This unit examines the extent of the influence of religion in contemporary Britain. It looks at the widely held view that religion is steadily declining in importance and influence in society.

Introduction

Surveys reveal that around 75% of the adult population in Britain claims to believe in God. This figure has remained fairly constant over the past 100 years. However, in the 1980s, less than 10% of the population attended church on Sunday, a figure that has steadily fallen over the past century. This unit considers one of the main issues in the sociology of religion: does declining church attendance demonstrate a decline in the influence of religion in society?

Secularization is the term given to the theory that the influence of religion in society is steadily diminishing. Thus, a secular society would be one in which religion was of little importance. Perhaps the most widely used definition of secularization in modern sociology has been provided by Bryan Wilson. This definition is reproduced below.

ACTIVITY 1

(a) Take the three separate elements of Wilson's definition (religious thinking; religious practice; and religious institutions), give examples of each and suggest how a decline in them might become apparent.

(b) Would a decline in one of these areas necessarily be matched by a decline in the others?

Photographs 7.2–7.4 indicate some of the points you could consider in addressing (a) and (b) above.

7.1
Wilson on secularization

Religious thinking, religious practices and religious institutions were once at the very centre of the life of western society, as indeed of all societies. That there were, even in the seventeenth, and certainly in the eighteenth and nineteenth, centuries many unchurched people to whom religious practices and places were alien and whose religious thinking was a mixture of odd piety, good intentions, rationalizations and superstitions, does not gainsay (contradict or deny) the dominance of religion. It was entrenched, if not always strictly by law, then by some of the institutions of society, in the customs of the people . . .

In the twentieth century that situation has manifestly changed, and the process of change continues . . .

. . . Religion – seen as a way of thinking, as the performance of particular practices, and as the institutionalization and organization of these patterns of thought and action – has lost influence in both England and the United States in particular, as it has in other western societies.

Source: B.R. Wilson *Religion in Secular Society*, Watts, London, 1966, pp. 9–11

7.2

Pope John Paul II receiving an ecstatic welcome in Canterbury, 1982

7.3

7.4

The new London mosque – an important centre for Muslims in Britain

The measurement of religion

ACTIVITY 2

(a) Consider and list possible ways by which secularization might be measured – data 7.5–7.9 might provide a starting point.

(b) Suggest the advantages and disadvantages of the various methods you have listed. Refer to data 7.5–7.9 in your answer.

7.5

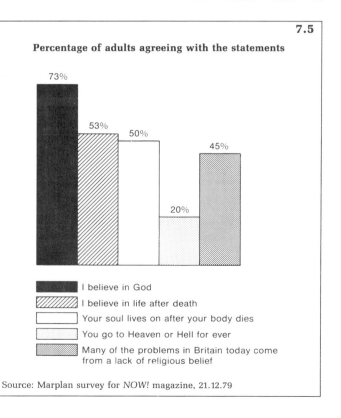

Percentage of adults agreeing with the statements

73%   53%   50%   20%   45%

- ▮ I believe in God
- ▨ I believe in life after death
- ▯ Your soul lives on after your body dies
- ▭ You go to Heaven or Hell for ever
- ▥ Many of the problems in Britain today come from a lack of religious belief

Source: Marplan survey for *NOW!* magazine, 21.12.79

7.6

Christian church membership in the UK

	1970	1985
Catholic	2,680,000	2,162,000
Anglican	2,548,000	1,984,000
Presbyterian	1,807,000	1,389,000
Methodist	601,000	436,000
Baptist	272,000	208,000
Other denominations	634,000	689,000
Total Christian membership	8,623,000	6,925,000
% of the adult population	20.4	15.2

Source: *Social Trends*, 1987

7.7

Infant baptisms in Britain

	1961	1979
Church of England	421,000	223,000
Catholic	131,000	76,000

Source: *Social Trends*, 1982

7.8

Marriages in Britain

	1966	1985
Church of England	175,000	116,000
Catholic	51,000	34,000
Register Office	138,000	185,000

Source: *Social Trends*, 1987

7.9

Lure of the Islamic Faith

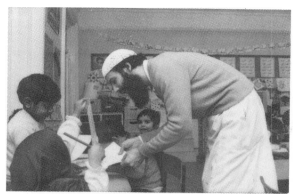

Yusuf Islam, ex-pop star Cat Stevens, teaching at his North London school.

In a wide and tree-lined North London street...is the Islamia Primary School. Islamic parents have been bringing a growing number of their children here since 1983 when a pop star called Cat Stevens, under his new name of Yusuf Islam, opened a kindergarten for Muslims...

When Yusuf Islam founded his school three years ago, most of the parents who approached him were from the Middle East and Pakistan. Converts are beginning to outnumber them. Each week at London's central mosque in St. John's Wood, some three or four Britons are professing their switch to Islam. On Fridays, at prayers, the British group now forms a visible and solid body. Extrapolated to the whole country, these numbers mean something like 5,000 new converts in the last five or six years.

Source: C. Moorhead, *The Times*, 25.9.85

Arguments for secularization

Although there is a widespread, general feeling that religion is less influential, there is by no means universal agreement among sociologists in support of the assumption and theory of secularization. We will look firstly at arguments for secularization and, secondly, at the arguments against the secularization theory.

ACTIVITY 3

List any evidence that you feel demonstrates the declining importance and influence of religion in society.

Data 7.10 and 7.11 provide examples of the changing role and nature of religion which you might wish to consider.

7.10

Come All Ye Faithful?

Nine a.m. on any school-day morning and thousands of Britain's head teachers are probably breaking the law. Not by embezzling the dinner money or viciously assaulting their pupils, but by failing to start the day with an act of worship attended by the whole school.

The Butler Education Act of 1944 revolutionized education in this country but the only legal requirements imposed on schools' time-tables were to give religious instruction and hold daily religious assemblies...The law has stood for 40 years but is now often ignored, not just in the spirit, but in the letter; school assembly no more than an irregular, desultory distribution of notices, and religion the dustiest subject on the timetable.

Source: M. Jay 'Come All Ye Faithful?' in *The Listener*, 20–27 December, 1984

7.11

A church converted into a radio station

Having looked at and discussed in general terms the supposed decline in the influence of religion, we now look at some more detailed arguments and accounts.

ACTIVITY 4
Read the extracts 7.12–7.14.

Consider and list how they might be used as support for the secularization theory. Look for any links or similarities between the passages.

7.12

The early Victorian era was essentially a religious age. Whether it was also more spiritual than earlier or succeeding ages is by no means so clear. . .

Probably the most striking difference in this respect between the early Victorian period and our own age was the extent of outward religious observance. In 1851, for the first and only time, an official census of attendance at all places of religious worship was taken. It showed that on Sunday, 30 March 1851, over seven million of the eighteen million inhabitants of England and Wales attended public worship. After allowing for young children, invalids and aged persons, and those who were occupied in household and other work on Sunday (totalling about 30 per cent of the population who could not attend church or chapel), it was estimated that about 60 per cent of possible worshippers attended.

Source: J.F.C. Harrison *The Early Victorians 1832–1851*, Weidenfeld and Nicolson, London, 1971, p. 150

7.13

It was the custom of most mid-Victorian Christians to proclaim that Britain was, essentially, a Christian country. . . The old maxim that 'Christianity is part of the law of England' still had some kick in it . . . National Days of Fasting and Humiliation were proclaimed in 1853 (cholera), 1854 (Crimea) and 1857 (Indian mutiny). The state of the law regarding 'the Lord's Day' hardly altered during our period . . . Excursion and other Sunday trains were never statutorily suppressed, but Sunday postal services were strictly reduced (1850) and so was the playing of military, though not private, bands in public parks. Theatres, pleasure grounds and all other places of entertainment charging for admission remained as closed as they had since 1781 . . .

Parliament daily opened business with prayers . . . Clergymen were called upon to add religious seriousness to every sort of public occasion, from prize-givings and cattle-shows to ratepayers' meetings and political protests.

Source: G. Best *Mid-Victorian Britain, 1851–1875*, Weidenfeld and Nicolson, London, 1971, pp. 191–194

7.14

As scientific orientations increase . . . so we can expect conceptions of society itself to become increasingly affected by rationalistic assumptions . . . Men are more and more involved in social activities in which their own emotional dispositions are less immediately relevant. Men may have become more rational . . . but perhaps even more important is their sustained involvement in rational organizations – firms, public service, educational institutions, government, the state – which impose rational behaviour upon them. The Churches with their dominant function as the institutionalization of emotional gratification, necessarily stand in sharp and increasingly disadvantageous contrast.

. . . The entertainment industry . . . was from the outset a challenge to religion, offering diversion, other reinterpretations of daily life, and competing for the time, attention and money of the public. In its actual content it may be seen as more than an alternative way of spending time, but also as an alternative set of norms and values. It replaced religion's attempt to awaken public sentiments by offering titillation of private emotions.

. . . The expansion of science and the fact that scientific operations 'proved themselves' in the eyes of the man in the street led to a new pragmatic test for all ideological systems. Science not only explained many facets of life and the material environment in a way more satisfactory than alternative religious interpretations, but it also provided confirmation of its explanation in practical results.

. . . Since science had answers . . . it came increasingly to command respect and approval.

Source: B.R. Wilson *Religion in Secular Society*, Watts, London, 1966, pp. 56–58

In modern Western societies a wide range of different forms of religion are tolerated. There is what is termed 'religious pluralism'. Rather than showing the continued importance of religion, it is argued that the tolerance of many different religions indicates a general indifference towards religion.

ACTIVITY 5
(a) Examine data 7.15–7.17 and then provide examples of the pluralism of religious beliefs in Britain.

(b) Can you suggest a possible alternative interpretation of this increasing diversity of religious beliefs?

7.15

Membership of non-Christian religions in the UK

	1970	1985
Muslims	250,000	853,000
Sikhs	75,000	185,000
Hindus	50,000	130,000
Jews	113,000	109,000
Jehovah's Witnesses	62,000	102,000

Source: *Social Trends*, 1987

7.16

Increasingly, as religious pluralism develops, the individual is forced to be aware of others who do not believe what he believes and who hold quite different meanings, values and beliefs. As a result this diversity of religious beliefs has a secularizing effect. That is, religious pluralism weakens the hold of religion on society and on the individual.

The most visible consequence of religious pluralism has been the privatization of religion. Although religion is less and less important in public, social life, it has successfuly maintained itself as an expression of private belief . . . Religious symbols still have an important place in private life . . . People continue to use religion for the great events of life, such as birth, marriage and death.

Source: adapted from Berger, P.L., Berger B. and Kellner, H. *The Homeless Mind*, Penguin, Harmondsworth, 1974, p. 75

7.17

Sikh Temple, Bradford

Arguments against secularization

ACTIVITY 6
List any evidence that you feel demonstrates the continuing importance and influence of religion in society. Refer to data 7.18–7.20 in your answer.

7.19

Casual observers of the religious scene have been induced over the past eight months or so to believe that the Church in the United Kingdom has changed: that it has deserted old rigours in favour of a new tendency towards political soft-heartedness . . . In May the Church of Scotland decided to allow the ordination of a man who had served time in prison for battering his mother to death. In October, Robert Runcie, the Archbishop of Canterbury, gave an interview to the religious affairs correspondent of the Times in order to deplore 'a movement from consensus to confrontation' that he detected in the nation's affairs. The background was by now a long-running miners' strike as well as heavy unemployment. In November mediation in that strike was attempted by a group of church leaders representing the Roman Catholic and United Reformed Churches as well as the Church of England . . .

Ideas about religion run most strongly when they have a symbol to accompany them; and the figure who has opportunely presented himself as a symbol of this imagined shift is David Jenkins . . . In his enthronement sermon in Durham in September, Jenkins said 'The miners must not be defeated', and spoke slightingly of Ian McGregor, the chairman of the National Coal Board.

Those last few interventions, in particular, were too much for John Selwyn Gummer, the chairman of the Conservative Party, who used a Cambridge sermon at the end of November to reprove bishops for political and doctrinal unsoundness.

Source: J. Whale 'The Church Militant and Visible', in *The Listener*, 20–27 December, 1984

7.18

Pope calls on world not to debase human life

The Pope waving to 300,000 pilgrims in St Peter's Square yesterday, after appealing to the world not to debase human life (Roger Boyes writes). The Pope's address reflected his concern about the immorality of abortion, contraception, artificial procreation and *in vitro* fertilization.

● **JERUSALEM:** Thousands of Christian pilgrims flocked to pray yesterday as church bells rang out (Reuter reports). Israeli soldiers carrying submachine-guns patrolled the Old City.

● **MOSCOW:** Thousands packed churches here on Saturday night and early yesterday to celebrate Easter, the main Russian Orthodox festival, but heavy police and civilian militia patrols kept many people away (Reuter reports).

● **COLOMBO:** Thousands prayed for peace in Sri Lanka yesterday as security forces hunted Tamil rebels who massacred 127 bus passengers on Friday (Reuter reports). Christians thronged churches and heard emotional sermons by priests who appealed for peace and an end to senseless killings.

● **MACAO:** The Portuguese Prime Minister, Senhor Aníbal Cavaço Silva, attended an Easter Mass yesterday where worshippers prayed for the territory's future (Reuter reports). About 2,000 people attended the Mass.

Source: *The Times*, 20.4.87

7.20

Radio Times

6.40 Songs of Praise from the big top at Funcoast World in Skegness. (Ceefax)
7.15 The Russ Abbot Show. (r) (Ceefax)
7.45 The District Nurse. Episode seven. (Ceefax)
8.40 Mastermind. The specialist subjects are: the first Austrian republic: F Scott Fitzgerald; Kenya 1890 to 1964; and the US Eighth Army in Europe, 1942 to 1945.
9.10 News and weather
9.25 Just Good Friends. Five years after they parted, Vince and Penny meet again. (Ceefax) (r)
9.55 Only Fools and Horses...Del's plans to make big money come a cropper once again. (r)
10.25 Heart of the Matter. How can the Roman Catholic Church in Northern Ireland, while tending to the needs of its flock, distance itself from the shadow of the Armalite rifle?
11.00 Video Active. Advice on making videos.
11.25 A Passion for Churches. (r) (see Choice)
12.15 Weather.

ACTIVITY 7

Having looked at general examples of the influence of religion, read the more detailed accounts, 7.21 and 7.22. List any common points or links you find between them and suggest the implications they might have for the secularization debate. (You could consider how they might be used in arguing that the theory of secularization cannot necessarily be accepted unquestioningly.)

7.22

Victorian religion – an alternative view

In the words of Horace Mann, the chief statistician (for the 1851 census), the 'labouring myriads, the masses of our working population...are never or but seldom seen in our religious congregations'. In rural areas and small towns a far greater proportion of the population attended church than in the cities. The places in which church-going was lowest included every large town described in the census report...Everywhere clergymen in towns and cities spoke of the difficulties of attracting mass support. According to Mann's calculations, fewer than one person in ten attended church or chapel on census day in Birmingham, Liverpool, Manchester, Sheffield and Newcastle. The metropolis, particularly in its crowded areas like Lambeth or Tower Hamlets, was equally indifferent to the call for regular worship. 'What is St. Paul's?' Henry Mayhew asked one of his London costermongers (fruit/vegetable sellers). 'A church, sir, so I've heard', was the reply. 'I never was in church'.

Source: A. Briggs *Victorian Cities*, Penguin, Harmondsworth, 1968, p. 63

7.21

TV evangelism

In 1980 the top five performers received a third of a billion dollars from television viewers. What began as rugged individualism has become a big industry...

Rex Hubbard is the doyen of television evangelists. For 30 years he videotaped his programmes from the Cathedral of Tomorrow in Akron, Ohio, a 5,000 seat auditorium purpose-built for television. Now he has retired to Florida and from the sub-tropical setting of Callaway Gardens produces and stars in his showbiz spectaculars...

His programmes are dubbed into nine languages and are transmitted on 400 television stations outside America...

The future of television evangelism is most dramatically symbolized by the Christian Broadcasting Network in Virginia Beach – acres and acres of building packed with the most advanced television technology and dominated by huge satellite dishes upturned to the heavens. GBN does not go in for formal religious services but gets the message across by using all the conventions of television – chat shows, drama, soap operas, cartoons and documentaries. All are of a high professional standard and are widely syndicated throughout America and beyond. CBN actually owns four TV stations and employs hundreds of technicians of one sort or another.

Source: C. Morris 'Will America's TV evangelists create a heretical substitute Church in Britain?' in *The Listener*, 12.1.84

TV evangelist Jimmy Swaggart

ACTIVITY 8

When we looked at the 'arguments for secularization', you were asked to think about the idea that religious pluralism could be used as an indicator of the declining importance of religion. Assess whether data 7.23 and 7.24 fit in with the notion that religious pluralism is linked to secularization, as suggested by Berger and colleagues (7.16)

7.23

A new religious consciousness?

Disenchantment with cultural, social and political arrangements accompanied by proposals for and experimentation with alternatives is not unique to the sixties, of course. Protest has been an abiding, if undulating, characteristic of American society since its founding . . . (However) the sixties, I am suggesting, were characterized by a crisis in consciousness unique in American history . . .

By the time of the sixties many Americans whose hopes and aspirations had been raised had become bitterly frustrated when things were not made considerably better for them . . . Thus, at the time of the outbreak of the youth rebellion there existed a widespread disenchantment with a social system that had failed to fulfil the hopes of a better society which the alternative world view had nurtured . . .

Some of the proposed alternatives called for a transformation of society. Marxism in many guises and Maoism were the most prominent of these . . . More frequently, the alternatives were characterized by solutions grounded in transformation of self . . . Religion – Eastern and Western – the occult, astrology, drugs and extra-sensory perception were the sources of other alternative realities. Some of the things tried worked for those who tried them, but there was no solution on which there was enough agreement to form a mass base for revolution, symbolic or real.

Source: C.Y. Glock 'Consciousness among Contemporary Youth: An Interpretation', in Glock, C.Y. and Bellah R.N. (eds.) *The New Religious Consciousness*, University of California Press, Berkeley, 1976

Within You Without You

The 'hippy movement of the 1960s was closely linked with the 'new religious consciousness', the search for new meanings and beliefs. Much of the contemporary music of the time reflected this interest. The following extract is taken from the lyrics on the Beatles' famous L.P. 'Sgt. Pepper's Lonely Hearts Club Band', released in 1967 at the height of the hippy movement.

'We were talking – about the love that's gone so cold and the people,
Who gain the world and lose their soul – they don't know – they can't see – are you one of them?
When you've seen beyond yourself – then you may find, peace of mind, is waiting there –
And the time will come when you see we're all one, and life flows on within you and without you.'

Source: *Within You and Without You* – George Harrison, 1967

7.24

The Beatles and Maharishi Mahesh Yogi

New religious movements and the secularization debate

From the material you have looked at so far, you will be aware that the new religious movements of the last twenty or so years can be viewed from two distinct perspectives: a) as evidence of the declining importance of religion in society (see data 7.16) b) as evidence of the birth of a 'new religiosity', especially among young people (see 7.23) The first three extracts (7.25–7.27) provide very different interpretations of the 'Moonies' (the Unification Church of Rev. Moon). This is probably the best known and most contentious and criticised of the new religions. It is interesting to compare the different ways in which the Moonies are portrayed by the different press accounts – the 'moral outrage' of the *Daily Mail* in contrast to the less emotive, more considered comments of the writers in *The Guardian* and *New Society*. The fourth extract (7.28) looks at a different type of new religious movement which stresses personal growth. Such movements are closely allied with some of the ideas and aspects of modern psychology (particularly psycho-therapy).

7.25

The aching void the religious cults seek to fill

How widespread are the cults in Britain and how dangerous? James Beckford, a sociologist of the new religions at Durham University, discounting the exaggerations of cults and anti-cults, doubts whether more than 15,000 people have been actively involved at any time in the last 15 years . . .

Academics and churchmen now refer to the cults, with respect, as 'new religious movements'. There is emerging agreement that their continuing appeal lies less in their own strength than in the weakness of society around them. Optimism, fellowship, love, laughter, hard work, and faith seem to find inadequate scope in families – whatever bereaved parents may imagine – in jobs, in politics, or in churches.

'I felt I had found my home at last,' a young Moonie told the sociologist Eileen Barker . . . 'I felt completely carefree for the first time in my life and a feeling of great hope for the future, not just for myself but for the whole world.'

Source: W. Schwarz *The Guardian* 11.20.85

7.26

Daily Mail wins historic libel action

THE DAMNING VERDICT ON THE MOONIES

By GORDON GREIG and TED OLIVER

THE Daily Mail was RIGHT to expose the Moonies quasi-religious sect as 'the church that breaks up families,' a High Court jury decided yesterday.

As a result, the Government is ordering a review of the Moonies, activities, including the effect of their psychiatric techniques on young members.

In the High Court, the jury delivered its verdict for the Mail after the longest and costliest libel case in British legal history, ruling that the Moonies' UK leader Dennis Orme had not been libelled by this newspaper.

And the six men and five women added two riders to their verdict. They urged that the charitable status of the Unification Church — The Moonies' official title — should be examined by the Inland Revenue on the grounds that it was really a political organisation: and they expressed their 'deep compassion' for all the young people still members of the sect.

Source: *Daily Mail*, 1.4.81

Mother's prayer

ANNE FYVIE'S daugher Lorne is 23 and gave up her law studies to become a Moonie nearly two years ago. Outside the court, Mrs Fyvie said: 'I don't think this decision will bring our daughter back, but hopefully it will help to save others. I hope that the authorities will act to stop these people and I pray that it is not too late for Lorne.'

7.27

The Making of a Moonie

Eileen Barker has probably seen more of the Moonies than even the average Moonie (since most of them leave within two years and she has been pursuing them for ten). She has spent endless hours with them, interviewing, observing, participating...She has tracked down people who left, people who tried the initial workshops and didn't like them...

And what does all this enterprise show? Well, for a start the Moonies don't eat so very differently from a great many students, or get fewer hours sleep than enables them to pass degree exams – and nobody can regard the average student as brainwashed other than in the universal and therefore vacuous sense that 'today everyone is brainwashed'. Secondly, no one who wishes to depart would suffer physically more than a modest inconvenience. Thirdly, out of over 1,000 people Moonies recruiters persuaded to attend a London two-day workshop in 1979, only 13 per cent affiliated with the Unification Church in any capacity, only 8 per cent joined as full-time members for more than one week, and less than 4 per cent remained in the church after two years. If this is 'brainwashing', as Barker clearly demonstrates, it is a remarkably inefficient process.

Source: R. Wallis 'Five Finger Exercise', a review of E. Barker's *The Making of a Moonie*, in *New Society* 19.11.84

Moonie instructors talk to recruits

7.28

In contrast to those new religions which drew heavily upon existing religious traditions, there also rose to prominence in the 1960s and 1970s a range of movements quite different in character, which seemed to owe more to the fringes of modern psychology than to the historic religious culture. Scientology is one such movement...Scientology offered a wide range of practice designed to enable an individual to achieve his full potential as a human being and ultimately as a spiritual entity...

Erhard Seminar Training (usually known as 'Est') also offered to provide a kind of enlightenment in a rather more rapid fashion and at substantially less cost than Scientology (from which, however, many of its ideas were derived). Est purveyed a 60 hour training taken over two weekends, the purpose of which was 'to transform your ability to experience living so that the situations you have been putting up with clear up just in the process of life itself'. This is clearly not the stuff of traditional religion.

Such movements typically place little emphasis on collective ritual or worship. They focus on the problems of individuals...Their practices are directed more to alleviating the problems of this life than to achieving salvation in some other worldly heaven...

Not only is the content of these movements' ideas and practices distant from that of traditional religion, but so, likewise, is their organizational form.

Rather than as churches or chapels, such movements typically organize themselves in the form of multi-national business corporations, with branch offices and a sales force. They employ the techniques of modern marketing and advertising providing their services with facilities for time payment or discounts for cash.

Source: R. Wallis 'The Sociology of the New Religions', in *Social Studies Review*, September 1985

Summary and conclusion

In this unit we have looked at information and arguments on the extent of religious belief and practice and the influence of religion in contemporary society. As should be apparent from examining this material, there are no straightforward answers. At the start of the unit it was stated that there was a generally held view that religion is less important, that we are becoming a secular society. Given the evidence you have looked at, it might be appropriate to ask yourself whether you feel that this evidence reinforces or refutes the popular view that we are a less religious society, or indeed, whether the concept of secularization is measurable at all.

It should be pointed out that we have used the notion of secularization, and the term itself, in a fairly unproblematic way. It could legitimately be asked whether secularization can be studied as a single concept. For instance, are religious attitudes and beliefs and formal, churchly religion of the same order? Can they be measured and discussed as one? It might clarify the issue to distinguish between (a) secularization of individual beliefs – where individuals lose interest in the supernatural and base their lives around purely rational means of organizing work and relationships and (b) secularization as it applies to religious institutions within society – where individuals might still believe in the supernatural but where the churches' authority and hold over the people is weakened.

It is the latter position which is perhaps nearer to the situation in modern societies such as Britain.

Further reading

Barker, E. *The Making of a Moonie*, Blackwell, Oxford, 1984
Gilbert, A.D. *The Making of Post-Christian Britain*, Longman, Harlow, 1980
Glock, C.Y. and Bellah, R.N. *The New Religious Consciousness*, University of California Press, Berkeley, 1976
Martin, D. *A General Theory of Secularization*, Blackwell, Oxford, 1978
Thompson, I. *Sociology in Focus: Religion*, Longman, Harlow, 1986

UNIT 8   Community

Most people have some connection to the place in which they live: relatives, neighbours, friends, or membership of clubs or organisations. But do these connections make up a 'community'? Many people would like to be part of a community yet there is a general belief that the process of community breakup is well underway. This unit explores the following question. Has there been a loss of community in Britain?

What is 'community'?

ACTIVITY 1
Look at the illustration below. Is it a picture of 'community' or of overcrowding and squalor?

Justify your answer.

8.1

The rear of terraced houses in London, engraving by Gustave Doré, 1872

Knowing a lot of people in a particular area may give an individual or family a sense of community. Data 8.2 contrasts close-knit and loose-knit social networks. Extract 8.3 from Young and Willmott's famous study of Bethnal Green in the East End of London shows the connection between family and social networks. Data 8.4 is based on research which looked at the difference made by the amount of traffic to the way inhabitants of some streets in San Francisco saw their lives.

ACTIVITY 2

(a) From data 8.2, briefly describe the difference between a close-knit and loose-knit social network.

(b) Using data 8.2, produce a diagram to illustrate your own social network, either as a family or as an individual.

(c) Compare your diagram with those in data 8.2. How would you describe your social network?

(d) Would you prefer your social network to be any different? Why or why not?

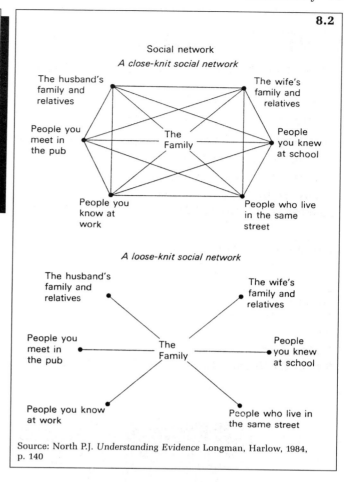

8.2

Social network
A close-knit social network

A loose-knit social network

Source: North P.J. *Understanding Evidence* Longman, Harlow, 1984, p. 140

ACTIVITY 3

(a) Read data 8.3. What kind of social network is being described here?

(b) How many people do you consider yourself to 'know' in the street in which you live? How does it compare with Mrs. Landon?

8.3

Connections on the street

'Some days,' says Mrs. Landon, 'you see so many you don't know which to talk to.' She kept a record over a week of all the people she knew in the street and who she considered herself to 'know'. There were 63 in all, some seen many times and 38 of them relatives of at least one other person of the 63. Her story showed that she had built up a series of connections with people she had known in school, work or street, and, even more forcefully, how her mother and other kin acted as a means of communication between herself and the other people in her social world.

Source: Young M. and Willmott P. *Family and Kinship in East London* Penguin, Harmondsworth, 1957

Images of community in the past

There is a certain nostalgia about the ideal of community based on close-knit social networks and hardships shared in common, often associated with a predominantly rural pre-industrial Britain. The period of rapid industrialisation and urbanisation last century had some impact on patterns of residence and, it is often assumed, disrupted life based on established, settled communities. However, historians are divided upon this view.

ACTIVITY 4

(a) In data 8.4, 'light', 'medium' and 'heavy' refer to amounts of traffic. What do these diagrams show about the impact of traffic on:
  (i) networks of social contacts,
  (ii) conceptions of personal territory in different streets?

(b) What do you think it would be like to live in each street?

(c) Which 'street' would you like to live in, and why?

(d) What do you think is the major influence on social contacts and personal territory in your street?

8.4

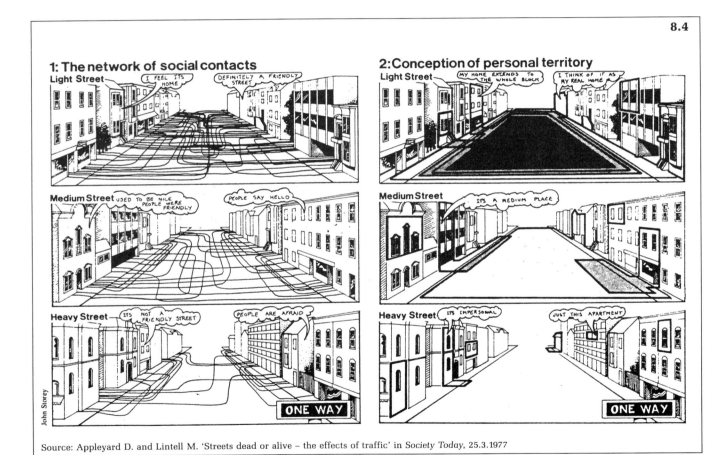

Source: Appleyard D. and Lintell M. 'Streets dead or alive – the effects of traffic' in *Society Today*, 25.3.1977

ACTIVITY 5

Data 8.5 is a summary of 94 sociological definitions of community. Using these, plus ideas you have developed from activities 1–4, devise a definition of community.

8.5

An analysis of 94 definitions of community

69 agree that community includes: social interaction, area, some ties or bonds in common.

14 definitions include some common characteristic, other than area.

15 defined community using a rural area.

Source: Bell C. and Newby H. *Community Studies* Allen and Unwin, London, 1971

ACTIVITY 6
(a) Contrast the images of community shown in data 8.6.

8.6

ACTIVITY 7
(a) Re-write Jones' description (8.8) of life in rural pre-industrial England from a dissenting point of view, perhaps as an aggrieved or disgruntled farm labourer. (Data 8.7 might give you some ideas.)

(b) According to data 8.9, what happened to social relations in the industrial towns? What reason is given for this change?

(c) As data 8.8 and 8.9 show, images of rural life tend to be positive, those of urban life negative. Why do you think this is so?

8.7

Village society had a recognised social order. The squire, his family and the vicar were the most important people locally. Farm labourers and others were expected to show respect for their social 'superiors', who were usually also their masters.

8.8

Village life

England had been a land of villages where people lived their whole lives, for few travelled more than a few miles. The local squire was normally a humane father figure to whom all turned for advice – after all, his family had occupied the manor for generations and he had the habit of forgetting that his tenants owed him rent if the harvest was bad. His wife and daughter would lead the social life of the area and visit the sick, perhaps teach in the Sunday School. There was a clear social division between the few wealthy families and the poor, but they all lived close to each other; rarely would one find a village where the poor all lived in one part. The village was a community in a very real sense, and its very smallness gave it its special character – a character that remained throughout Victorian England, despite the Great Changes (i.e. industrialisation and urbanisation).

Source: Jones R.B. Economic and Social History of England, Longman, Harlow, 1971

8.9

Town life

Instead of the close-knit community of the villages, classes were divided by their earning power. It was in the towns that class war arose and it was this that led Karl Marx to develop his theory of the communist revolution. Many writers, perhaps sentimentally, deplored the passing of village community life. Carlyle put the point clearly, 'Our life is not a mutual helpfulness... it is a mutual hostility. We have profoundly forgotten everywhere that Cash-payment is not the sole relation of human beings; we think... that is absolves and liquidates all engagements of man.'

Source: Jones R.B. Economic and Social History of England, Longman, Harlow, 1971

The impact of housing programmes on inner city communities

As well as the impact of industrialisation and urbanisation last century and the continuing changes in the location of work this century, government housing programmes have been blamed for breaking up communities. Young and Willmott, in their study of Bethnal Green quoted in data 8.3, looked at the impact on family and community of the rehousing of working class families from the East End of London in suburban housing projects. Young and Willmott believed that the thoughtless destruction of established social networks led to a great deal of personal unhappiness and high social costs. Their ideas were not accepted until the late 1960s, when it was perhaps too late. 'If the lessons had been learned in the 1950s,' they say now, 'London and the other British cities might not have suffered the "anomie" and violence manifested in the urban riots of the 1980s.'

ACTIVITY 8

(a) Do you agree or disagree with the above quote from Willmott and Young? Give reasons for your answer.

(b) Describe how you might feel if you were one of the people in data 8.10 and 8.11? Refer in particular to your 'sense of community'.

8.10

HOME IS WHERE YOUR HEART IS

'They'll never get me up in one of those things.'

8.11

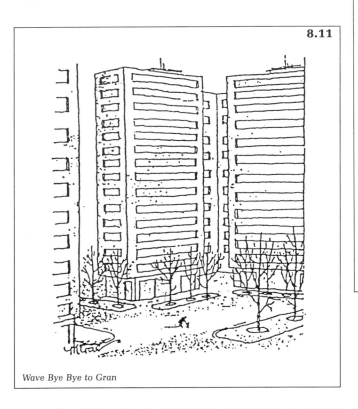

Wave Bye Bye to Gran

ACTIVITY 9

(a) What view does Orwell take of slum clearance? (8.12 and 8.13)

(b) Many people were rehoused in peripheral council housing estates, like Greenleigh, as well as the infamous high rise flats in the cartoons. In view of these factors, explain the possible reasons for the nostalgia noted by Campbell. (8.13)

(c) What happened to contact with relatives when Bethnal Greeners moved 20 miles away to Greenleigh? (8.14). Suggest reasons for the changes.

8.12

As you walk though the industrial towns you lose yourself in the labyrinths of little brick houses blackened by smoke, festering in planless chaos round miry alleys and little cindered yards where there are stinking dustbins and lines of grimy washing and half ruinous w.c.'s . . . at their very worst the Corporation (council) houses are better than the slums they replaced.

Source: Orwell G. *The Road to Wigan Pier* Penguin, Harmondsworth, 1937

8.13

The landscape George Orwell saw when he wandered round the backyard of England is a scene that still inhabits people's memory, though memory incites nostalgia about those 'cruel habitations'. People associate them with community spirit and sunshine, the days when 'we had nothing but were happy'.

Source: Campbell B. *Wigan Pier Revisited* Virago, London, 1984

8.14

Greenleigh

Less than 20 miles away from Bethnal Green, the automatic doors of the tube train open on to the new land of Greenleigh. On the one side of the railway are cows at pasture. On the other, the new housing estate. Greenleigh is fairly typical of the council estates to which many Bethnal Greeners have been moved. The changes in frequency of contact with relatives after moving to Greenleigh are outlined in the following table.

Changes in weekly contacts with relatives after moving to Greenleigh			
	Average no. of contacts per week with own spouse's parents and siblings		
	Before leaving Bethnal Green	*Greenleigh 1953*	*Greenleigh 1955*
Husbands	15.0	3.8	3.5
Wives	17.2	3.0	2.4

...In Bethnal Green, the kindred are at hand every day of the week. At Greenleigh the family has to wait for summer, for weekends, for holidays, before they appear.

Source: Young M. and Willmott P. *Family and Kinship in East London* Penguin, Harmondsworth, 1957

Locality and community

This section examines data from three more recent studies of local populations in England. Pahl's study looks at class and community in an English commuter village, with the fictional name of 'Dormersdell', in Hertfordshire. Pryce was a participant observer for four years in his study of St. Paul's in Bristol, a predominantly black inner city area. Holme revisited the East End areas studied by Young and Willmott.

'Dormersdell', Hertfordshire

ACTIVITY 10

(a) What does Pahl mean (8.15) when he says, 'the geographical and social divisions were mutually reinforcing'? Refer to the statistics at the start of the extract in your answer.

(b) According to Pahl, what was the basis of local village community life, before the 'invasion' of middle-class people?

(c) Similar changes have occured in some urban areas, a process known as 'Gentrification.' Is there a village or part of a town/city near you where changes in the social class of residents is obvious? If so, briefly describe the area.

8.15

Class of heads of household in areas of 'Dormersdell'					
	m/c	w/c	agric.	no info.	number
'The Wood'	92%	1%	1%	5%	65
'The Village'	39%	45%	13%	4%	77

Because of the peculiar geographical circumstances of 'Dormersdell', it is possible to discern a certain ecological segregation of the population according to socio-economic status. The preceding table shows the social composition of the two areas – the one centred round the old village centre and the other based on the area of woodland with the lanes leading to it. The geographical and social divisions were mutually reinforcing.

...(Pahl concludes) The middle-class people come into rural areas in search of a meaningful community and by their presence help to destroy whatever community was there. That is not to say that the middle-class people change or influence the working-class. They simply make them aware of national class divisions, thus polarizing the local society. Part of the basis of the local village community was the sharing of the deprivations due to the isolation of country life and the sharing of the limited world of the families within the village. The middle-class people try to get the 'cosiness' of village life, without suffering any of the deprivations, and while maintaining a whole range of contacts with the outside world by means of the greater mobility afforded by their private transport.

Source. Pahl R.E. *Whose City?* Longman, Harlow, 1970

St. Paul's, Bristol

ACTIVITY 10

(a) Why does St. Paul's give the impression of being a 'community' to outsiders?

(b) According to Pryce, why do 'students and intellectuals' fail to recognise the lack of community in St. Paul's?

(c) What evidence is provided by data 8.16 and 8.17 to suggest that St. Paul's not only lacks the cohesion of a community but also contains divisions which may result in discord and conflict?

8.16

Life-style map – St. Paul's

BRISTOL

Sub-proletarian Employment | Sub-proletarian Employment

Impact | Impact

REPLACEMENT POPULATION | REPLACEMENT POPULATION

WORK SITUATION IN WEST INDIAN COMMUNITY

THOSE WHO DON'T WORK | BI-NORMATIVE RESPONSES | THOSE WHO WORK

Expressive-Disreputable Orientation | Stable Law-abiding Orientation

REJECTION OF 'SLAVE LABOUR' AND 'SHIT WORK' | ACCOMMODATION TO 'SLAVE LABOUR' AND 'SHIT WORK'

'HUSTLES' | 'SLAVE LABOUR'

Hustlers | Teenyboppers | Proletarian Resp's | Saints | In-bet-weeners | Main-liners

Predominantly white-collar workers, but confined to the race relations industry, etc.

Bur-geoning lower class or lumpenproletariat | Pre-dominantly working class

World-views and political attitudes

(1) *Hustlers* (first generation refusers of 'slave labour' and 'shit work') = hedonistic, criminalistic and indifferent to white society.

(2) *Teenyboppers* (second generation refusers of 'slave labour' and 'shit work') = delinquency, Rastafarianism and other forms of black consciousness.

World-views and political attitudes (mixed)

(3) *Pro. Resp's* = God-fearing, peaceful accommodation.

(4) *Saints* = Pentecostalist, peaceful accommodation.

(5) *In-betweeners* = black people conscious and anti-integrationist.

(6) *Mainliners* = pro-liberal and conservative-moderate.

REPLACEMENT POPULATION

Source: Pryce K. *Endless Pressure* Penguin, Harmondsworth, 1979

8.17

Diversity and division

In his study of St. Paul's in Bristol, a predominantly black area, Pryce identifies six 'life-styles' under two main 'life orientations' or 'walks of life', as data 8.17 shows.

Pryce comments: 'The lack of community in St. Paul's is often not apparent to strangers visiting the area for the first time, especially students and intellectuals with their tendency to romanticize the deviant and the exotic. Diverse groups with vastly dissimilar backgrounds do mingle freely in close physical interaction in St. Paul's. But this is deceptive, for mingling of this kind does not automatically create a community spirit in the sense of conformity, consensus, and vigilance about community standards. The only unity is an external one, in the form of common services utilized by all. Beneath the romantics' illusion of a tight-knit, friendly, organic, warm, harmonious community, the divisions are deep. There is much suspicion between groups.'

Source: Pryce K. *Endless Pressure* Penguin, Harmondsworth, 1979

St. Paul's Festival – *an illusion of community?*

Bethnal Green, London

ACTIVITY 11

(a) Holme points to the 'home-centredness' of most Bethnal Green families. What does that mean? Why might it have happened?

(b) Does this 'home-centredness' mean that people don't have much contact with their friends, relatives and neighbours?

(c) Refer back to data 8.3 and contrast Holme's description with that of Young and Willmott.

Bethnal Green revisited
8.18

One striking difference was how home-centred most Bethnal Green families had now become. In the 1950s, this had been a feature of the Woodford families ['Woodford' is a middle class suburb in London studied by Willmott and Young in the 1950s.] But whatever the draw towards home, or occupation within it, the corollary in Bethnal Green to this new home-centredness was the emptiness of the streets and corridors and staircases in the housing estates. Markets still flourished. Children sometimes played outside. Small groups of adults occasionally congregated. But no longer could it be said that people in Bethnal Green were (in Young and Willmott's words) 'vigorously at home in the streets.' But though this relative emptiness now seems to approach that of Woodford, it is not of a similar order. [In Woodford much remains as it was in the 1950s, in fact Holme comments that, '. . . If anything, it is more neighbourly and friendly'.]

Source. Holme A 'Family and Homes in East London', *New Society*, 12.7.1985

The fight for community – the miners' strike of 1984–85

Mining settlements are often held up as examples of 'real' communities and in one sense the miners' strike of 1984–85 was about the fight for the survival of such communities. As the basis of life in many mining communities was working at the pit, the loss of jobs would obviously threaten a whole way of life. The extract from Goodman's book (8.19) illustrates this idea.

ACTIVITY 13

(a) Using your definition of community (from Activity 5) would you say mining settlements constitute 'communities'? Explain your answer.

(b) Suggest reasons why miners and their families tend to form close-knit communities.

(c) List arguments for and against maintaining such settlements.

Mining communities
8.19

The fact remains that mining villages and towns have always felt themselves to be part of a 'special breed' of working people and in a much stronger way than other groups, not least because of their earlier isolation in pit villages. If, in the majority of instances, this is no longer the case, then it has yet to be recognised as such by most miners and their families.

Pointing to the reliance on one main form of male employment in mining communities, Goodman quotes from a recent study by Fothergill and Gudgin: 'Coalfield communities have a distinctive employment structure. In 1981, the most recent date for which local employment statistics are available, coal provided just under 30% of the jobs for the men.' Obviously there are also ancillary trades and services so that the loss of a working pit in a village would be 'devastating'. Certainly a great deal of support was shown for miners, sometimes from some unlikely places, but more often locally.

In South Wales, local banks, building societies, shopkeepers and tradesmen advanced hundreds of thousands of pounds of credit. Similar credit facilities were common in Yorkshire, in the Northeast and in Scotland. A social worker in South Yorkshire told me, at the turn of 1985, that she had never seen such community spirit, such co-operation, such self-sacrifice in 25 years of social work in various parts of Britain. 'The miners' strike,' she told me, 'has brought out a spirit among people that is difficult to understand unless you have personally experienced it. It is rather like a religious experience.'

Source: Goodman G. *The Miners' Strike* Pluto Press, London, 1985

Welsh mining village

Community and social policy

Numerous government programmes use the notion of contract and liason between officialdom and the 'community' and the idea of generation or re-generation of the community as a potential solution (often acknowledged as partial) to the problems found in an area. As Pahl points out; '... priests, social workers and teachers frequently use the word "community". As a notion it is generally held to be "a good thing", particularly when it has a spirit attached to it. Social leaders and public persons are usually very ready to pass judgements on the quantities of this spirit that they can detect. Local groups are congratulated when they have lots of it. In other words, the notion of community or community spirit is value-loaded; people who use this phrase make certain tacit assumptions, which as sociologists we need to make explicit.'
The examples of policies/programmes in this section illustrate assumptions made about society and the role of government workers.
The Community Development Project (CDP) was set up in 1969. It was part of the poverty programmes of that time but there was also a clear social control element to the programme, as data 8.20 shows. The story of Devon and Cornwall's 'Community Policing' alternative has been frequently told. John Alderson (the chief constable) attempted to emphasise the social work aspect of policing and a preventative approach to crime. Some social work is based on a locality, identified as 'deprived' and there are a variety of community workers and community based programmes.

ACTIVITY 13

(a) Acording to data 8.20, why were CDP's set up?

(b) How could adventure playgrounds, playschemes and in later years, intermediate treatment projects (for young offenders) help to achieve the aims of CDP's?

(c) From your wider sociological study; what other factors would influence the problems which led to CDP's being set up?

8.20

Community Development Project

It is clear that, within Home Office thinking, the family and crime were inextricably linked. The rising rate of delinquency was an indication that the family was failing in its task of rearing law abiding citizens. In addition to improving the methods of dealing with offenders themselves through the police and courts, new ways had to be found to tackle the problem at source ... Established as an experiment in new ways of helping the family, (CDP) was to use the 'community' as a focus for mobilising informal social control mechanisms, rather than the individual or family in isolation. The police were involved in the planning stages of the Project and were prepared to work closely with it when established.

(Projects) ... ranged from adventure playgrounds and playschemes to, in later years, intermediate treatment projects and other alternatives to residential treatment for young offenders. The theme of family and community support was closely intertwined with another: race, racial tension, and race relations were a constant refrain in Home Office poverty projects, and for similar reasons. Racial tension can lead to violence and disorder while unemployed black teenagers might seek to take out their frustrations on white society.

Source: CDP Guilding the Ghetto – the state and poverty experiments

ACTIVITY 14

(a) List the various ways the term 'community policing' is used.

(b) What point is Alexei Sayle (8.22) making about community policing?

(c) What are the problems in implementing community policing? Refer to data 8.23 in your answer.

Community policing

8.21

The fact that community policing means such different things to different police forces is one reason why it is dangerous to regard it as a panacea. In some forces the term is applied to a community contact, liason or relations branches which have a purely specialist task of making links with local people. Their job is essentially to give the police a good name. They themselves are sometimes divided by their colleagues who meanwhile get on with the 'real policing'.

In other forces, community policing can mean that resident constables are deployed, more or less full-time (though how much more and how much less is an important variable) in a particular locality, normally a housing estate. Their job involves chatting up local residents and making themselves available but these officers still have a fairly traditional policing function, keeping tabs on the locals on behalf of the force at large and pulling them in if there is any trouble. In yet other areas, community policing may simply mean that officers walk or cycle from the local police station where once they glided around in cars. The Devon and Cornwall version with its emphasis on concerted local initiatives, devolved decision making and its greater involvement in the force as a whole, is quite different again. All that glistens is not community policing.

Source: Kettle M. and Hodges L. *Uprising* Pan, London, 1982

8.22

ROUND OUR WAY WE'VE GOT COMMUNITY POLICING. YOU'RE WALKING ALONG THE STREET, A POLICE VAN PULLS UP, A SQUAD OF COPPERS LEAP OUT, PIN YOU TO THE GROUND AND TELL YOU THE TIME

Alexei Sayle

8.23

'They had this community policeman around after the Scarman Report in 1981. John Beck was his name, and he was a nice bloke, who wanted to come here, but he said all the other community coppers were sent here from other forces for misdemeanours. They did try to get to know people but it was terribly embarrassing. They would come up and shake hands with you in the street, in front of the brothers, and you're thinking, Christ, I'm going to get killed as some kind of informer.'

[Quote from Gilbert Akinyele, a local community worker in Brixton.]

Source: Harris M. 'Looking back on the riot', *New Society*, 4.10.85

ACTIVITY 15

(a) Explain the role of community social worker.

(b) If 'real communities' existed, there would be no need for community social workers. Discuss briefly.

(c) Choose a specific 'social problem' requiring a community social worker. Using data 8.24 and 8.25, devise an advertisement for the type of worker required.

(d) Do you think the appointment will solve the social problem you have selected? Give reasons for your answer.

Community social work

8.24

Some social workers, aware of the effect of deprived environments, are drawn into work with neighbourhoods, and with minority groups within the community... These community workers often operate from projects which enable them to identify especially closely with the communities with whom they work, and act with them in negotiations with social services or social work departments as well as with many other statutory agencies.

Community workers operate with tenants associations and other groups on housing estates, in redevelopment areas, in New Towns and in multi-racial neighbourhoods. Community work emphasises the worker's contribution in sharing his knowledge and skills with deprived and relatively powerless groups of people so that they are enabled to tackle their problems, summon resources, participate in the life of the community, and cultivate a better quality of life.

The main task of some other community workers is to facilitate co-operation either between voluntary organisations, or between the local authority and such bodies.

Source: C.C.E.T.S.W. Information Service *Introducing Social Work* leaflet number 1:4, 1976

8.25

LEICESTER COMMUNITY PROJECT

COMMUNITY SOCIAL WORKER

Salary: £8,154 – £9,591 (with assessment at £8,697)

This project, situated in the Highfields District, an inner city area of high social need with a large multi-cultural population, is concerned with developing work with groups and individuals in the community. It uses a variety of approaches to help parents to realise their own potential and to cope with both their children and their own lives.

This is a key appointment. The successful applicant will be influential in the development of the project and new initiatives. The postholder will need to possess group work skills. Knowledge and/or experience of working with under 5s and their parents, and of Asian and/or Afro-Caribbean communities are also essential. A qualification in youth and community or social work is highly desirable.

The Church of England Children's Society is a Christian organisation which seeks in staff a readiness to grow in Christian faith and life.

For informal discussion/visit, telephone Val Fisher (0533-736536).

For application form/job description contact: Regional Office, 98 Church Hill Road, Handsworth, Birmingham B20 3PD. (A4 s.a.e. appreciated.)

Closing date for receipt of completed application forms: 14th February, 1986.

The Children's Society.

Conclusion

This unit has tried to give some meaning to the concept of community. The earlier sections looked at the changes in society which have either split up and dispersed people or divided them within localities. The strong thread of belief in the value of living in a community is partly behind the various policies developed to deal with some of society's social problems. But, as the final section has illustrated to some extent, a belief in the value of community is not the only issue at stake.

ACTIVITY 16

(a) Does the evidence in this unit suggest a stronger sense of community in the past?

(b) What are the advantages and disadvantages of a community-based way of life?

(c) List the factors which have led to the splitting up of some communities and the factors which divide some localities.

(d) Where would you expect to find people with a strong sense of living in a community today?

(e) Can we recreate or rebuild a community-based life in the future?

Further reading

Bell C. and Newby H. *Community Studies*, George Allen & Unwin, London, 1971
Lee D. and Newby H. *The Problem of Sociology* Hutchinson, London, 1983
Newby H. *Green and Pleasant Land? Social Change in Rural England* Penguin, Harmondsworth, 1980
Slattery, M. 'Urban Sociology' in *Sociology: New Directions*, M. Haralambos (ed.) Causeway, Ormskirk, 1985
The Economist *Britain's Urban Breakdown* 1982

UNIT 9   Patterns in Suicide

Much sociological theorising has been based on statistical information collected by government agencies. The aim of this unit is to investigate the adequacy of this kind of evidence.

ACTIVITY 1

(a) For which sex are there more suicides?

(b) What is the relationship between suicide and age?

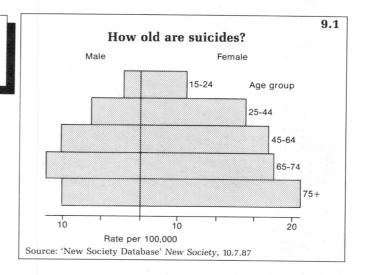

9.1

How old are suicides?

Male   Female

Age group: 15-24, 25-44, 45-64, 65-74, 75+

Rate per 100,000   10   10   20

Source: 'New Society Database' *New Society*, 10.7.87

Patterns in the statistics: the problem

The pattern you have just described is something which has persisted in England, Wales and Scotland for 100 years. This unit deals with the question of why there are such patterns in suicide statistics.

ACTIVITY 2
Write down what you think causes people to commit suicide. You can add to this list while you are doing Activity three.

ACTIVITY 3
Look at data 9.1–9.5 and complete the passage below. Note anything else you find interesting.

The evidence shows that suicide is most, likely among: males/females, aged ... of ... (social class), living in ... , using ... (method). It is least common among ... (age groups). Female suicides are most common between the ages of ... and ... Over the historical period 1900–1980 the highest suicide rates for males were between 19 ... and 19 ... Recently the most significant change in the suicide rate has been for ... (sex), aged ... , although overall the suicide rate has ...

9.2

Suicide Rates for Urban and Rural Areas
Suicides per 100,000

	Men		Women	
	1959–63	1970–72	1959–63	1970–72
Conurbations	15.7	10.3	10.7	7.6
Urban areas				
100,000 +	14.5	9.9	9.9	6.5
50,000–100,000	14.0	9.0	10.4	7.5
Under 50,000	13.6	8.3	8.6	5.7
Rural areas	11.8	9.4	6.4	5.3
England and Wales	14.1	9.5	9.3	6.5

Source: figures based upon *Suicides 1961–74*, published by the Office of Population Censuses and Surveys.

9.3

Suicide and social class

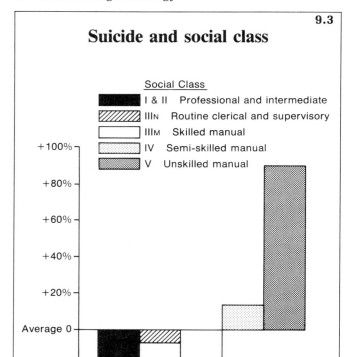

Suicide rates by social class; males 20–60; England and Wales;
above and below average.
Source: based on Table GD40, Decennial Review, *Occupational
Mortality* 1979–80 and 1982–83, OPCS

9.4

How people commit suicide

England and Wales, 1960-1973 Rates per 100,000

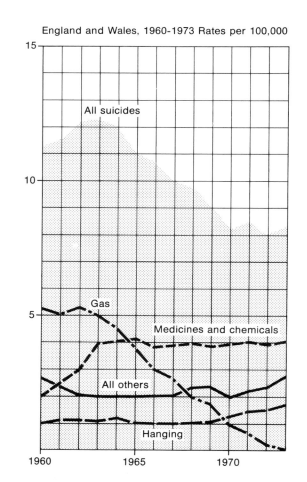

Source: 'New Society Database' *New Society*, 10.7.87

9.5

**Suicide rates per million by selected age groups, 1901–78, England
and Wales** (Five year averages 1901–05 and 1971–75. Three-year
average 1976–78)

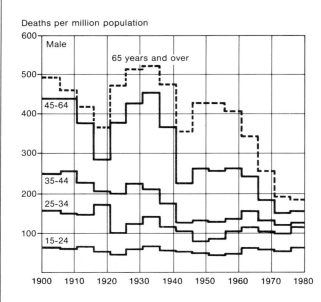

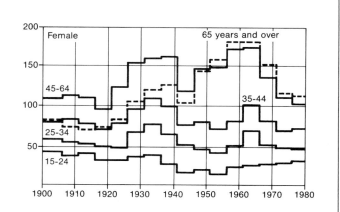

Source: *Suicide and Deliberate Self-harm*, Office of Health Economics, 1981, p. 10

ACTIVITY 4
Compare the ideas you listed in Activity 2 with what you discovered looking at the statistics. How far do the statistics provide evidence for or against your original ideas about the causes of suicide? What further data would you require to check out your ideas.

Patterns in suicide: possibilities

Activity 3 asked you to search the statistics for patterns. But why are there patterns in the statistics? There are three possible reasons.

1. It may be that the patterns in the statistics reflect something about the psychological make-up human beings are born with. Then the data might suggest that males are born more prone to suicide than females, or that increasing suicide proneness is part of a biological process of ageing. This is a PSYCHO-BIOLOGICAL kind of explanation.

2. It may be that the patterns in the statistics reflect something about the way in which society is organised to make some kinds of people more prone to suicide than others. Then the data would be telling us that there is something about the social life of males (especially of lower-class, elderly males) which makes them commit suicide more frequently. This is a sociological kind of explanation which relates the individual's psychological state and behaviour to the social structure: a SOCIO-STRUCTURAL EXPLANATION.

3. Maybe the patterns in the statistics are there because of the way in which deaths are classified and statistics collected and published: an ARTIFACT EXPLANATION.

ACTIVITY 5
(a) If patterns of suicide are similar from society to society, does this favour a psycho-biological explanation, or a socio-structural explanation?

(b) Look at data 9.6 and 9.7, and compare it with the evidence on suicide in the UK (9.1–9.5). What kind of explanation for suicide does all the evidence favour?
Give reasons for your answer.

9.6

The Aguaruna

[Among the Aguaruna of the Amazonian forest] suicide is...predominantly, although by no means exclusively, a female act...In general...male victims tend to be in their teens, female victims in teens and early 20's. The range of variability is much greater for women than it is for men, however; suicides of women in their 40's or 50's are not unknown, but in the sample there is not a single case of a middle-aged man killing himself.

Source: M. F. Brown 1986 'Power, gender the social meaning of Aguaruna suicide', *Man* 21:2 p. 313.

9.7

Western Samoa suicide rates/100,000 by age group and sex 1981–1983, inclusive

	Males	Females
0–14	0.91	2.0
15–24	71.0	40.9
25–34	76.0	20.4
35–44	44.2	10.9
45 +	15.4	0

Source: after MacPherson, C. & L. 1987 'Towards an Explanation of Recent Trends in Suicide in Western Samoa' *Man* 22:2 p. 309

Durkheim, suicide & scientific sociology

Emile Durkheim (1858–1917), one of the founding fathers of sociology, proposed a socio-structural theory of suicide. He chose the topic of suicide to illustrate his claim that sociology could be a scientific discipline. He made two kinds of claim for the scientific status of sociology:

1. That there is something real called 'society' for sociologists to study: something which governs individual behaviour.

2. That this real thing called society can be studied using the same rigorous methods as were being developed by the natural and physical scientists of his day.

The reality of society

Society is not something you can see directly: it doesn't seem to be like the rocks or the trees or the stars studied by natural scientists. What you can see are individuals and their behaviour, and the results of their behaviour such as building, books and motorcars. It may seem difficult to subject something you can't see directly to scientific study. But this is not something which bothers natural scientists.

Climatology is a scientific enterprise. But you can't actually see a climate. What you can see, feel and measure are rainfall, windspeed, air-pressure, temperature and such like. What we mean by 'climate' is the fairly regular patterns which emerge when we have measured and recorded meteorological phenomena.

Similarly a social scientist can argue that while we cannot directly see society we can observe and measure individual behaviour. The reality of society is shown in regular patterns that these records of individual behaviour show. For Durkheim the patterns in suicide statistics are evidence of a real society causing individual behaviour. The logic of Durkheim's approach is identical to the logic of the natural scientist.

THE WAY CLIMATE WORKS
|
governs
|
the rainfall, temperature etc.
|
therefore if you study the regularities in rainfall, temperature etc., you will understand how climates work.

THE WAY SOCIETY WORKS
|
governs
|
individual behaviour
|
therefore if you study the regularities in individual behaviour you will understand how society works.

ACTIVITY 6
Read data 9.8.
In what way does Durkheim argue that 'society' has a real existence over and above individuals?

9.8
Society and individuals

The individuals making up a society change from year to year, yet the number of suicides is the same so long as the society itself does not change. The population of Paris renews itself very rapidly: yet the share of Paris in the total of French suicides remains practically the same. Although only a few years suffice to change completely the personnel of the army, the rate of military suicides varies only very slowly within a given nation. The causes . . . must be independent of individuals, since they retain the same intensity no matter what particular persons they operate on.

Source: Durkheim E. *Suicide*, 1897, p. 307

Durkheim and the scientific method

In activities 1, 3 & 4 you did much as Durkheim did in his study of suicide. Durkheim also started with suicide statistics, looked for patterns in them, tried to find explanations for those patterns and tested out his hunches by looking at more data, or the same data in a different way. This approach is called the 'HYPOTHETICO-DEDUCTIVE METHOD', or simply 'the scientific method'. Some argue that only those activities which use this method can truly be called 'sciences'.

ACTIVITY 7
Study data 9.9
(a) In terms of the statistics on suicide rates, is the hypothesis confirmed? Give reasons for your answer.

(b) Think carefully about your answer to part (a). Can you think of anything about the data and/or your reasoning which might lead you to change your mind?

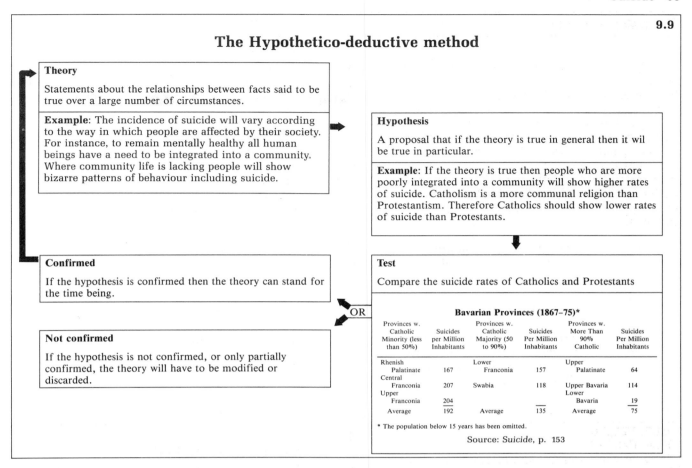

9.9

The Hypothetico-deductive method

Theory

Statements about the relationships between facts said to be true over a large number of circumstances.

Example: The incidence of suicide will vary according to the way in which people are affected by their society. For instance, to remain mentally healthy all human beings have a need to be integrated into a community. Where community life is lacking people will show bizarre patterns of behaviour including suicide.

Hypothesis

A proposal that if the theory is true in general then it wil be true in particular.

Example: If the theory is true then people who are more poorly integrated into a community will show higher rates of suicide. Catholism is a more communal religion than Protestantism. Therefore Catholics should show lower rates of suicide than Protestants.

Confirmed

If the hypothesis is confirmed then the theory can stand for the time being.

Not confirmed

If the hypothesis is not confirmed, or only partially confirmed, the theory will have to be modified or discarded.

Test

Compare the suicide rates of Catholics and Protestants

OR

Bavarian Provinces (1867–75)*

Provinces w. Catholic Minority (less than 50%)	Suicides per Million Inhabitants	Provinces w. Catholic Majority (50 to 90%)	Suicides Per Million Inhabitants	Provinces w. More Than 90% Catholic	Suicides Per Million Inhabitants
Rhenish Palatinate	167	Lower Franconia	157	Upper Palatinate	64
Central Franconia	207	Swabia	118	Upper Bavaria	114
Upper Franconia	204			Lower Bavaria	19
Average	192	Average	135	Average	75

* The population below 15 years has been omitted.

Source: *Suicide*, p. 153

Operationalising terms

Look critically at the reasoning in data 9.9. It relies on two main assumptions which may be questioned. Firstly, is it indeed true that Catholicism is a more communal religion than Protestantism? This in turn raises the question of what is meant by such terms as 'communal', 'community', 'integration' and so on. Secondly, taking the facts at face value, is it the alleged communal nature of Catholicism which produces the lower suicide rate, or some other difference between Catholics and Protestants? For example suicide is generally regarded as more sinful by Catholics than by Protestants.

The problem here is one of 'operationalisation'. In the example Catholicism is made to stand for 'more communal', and Protestantism for less. Degrees of community are operationalised in terms of religious affiliation. A hypothesis is only as good as the way it operationalises a theory.

The following section examines how Durkheim operationalises suicide.

Suicide and social control: Durkheim's theory

Durkheim relates suicide rates to the way in which a society controls its members. He proposes two kinds of social control. 'Social Solidarity' is the extent to which an individual is incorporated into a community: the extent to which he or she acts independently or acts under pressure from a group. 'Social Regulation' is the degree to which people's lives are controlled by ideas given them by their membership of society, or the extent to which they work things out for themselves.

In terms of Durkheim's theory too much social control or too little causes high rates of suicide.

ACTIVITY 8

In terms of Durkheim's categories (9.10) what kind of suicide is the following?

An officer in the army has been charged with cowardice in the face of the enemy. Left alone before his trial he shoots himself with his pistol.

Now add the following to the case and see where it fits into Durkheim's classification of suicide. We think you'll find it very difficult.

(i)   The officer is a very loyal member of his regiment and wishes to avoid dishonouring it by going through with the trial.

(ii)   The officer is completely devastated by his predicament. The bottom has fallen out of his world. He cannot bear the uncertainty of awaiting the outcome of the trial.

(iii) The officer is certain he will be found guilty and shot. It is easier for him to shoot himself rather than to be put to the additional ordeal of the trial.

(iv)   The officer has been persuaded by his commanding officer that if he 'does the right thing' he will be listed as having died during active service. His name will not be dishonoured and his relatives will receive a pension.

Anomic, egoistic, altruistic, fatalistic suicide, or some combination of these?

Durkheim's types of suicide

9.10

Egoistic suicide – social solidarity low

'results from the fact that society is not sufficiently integrated at all points to keep its members under control . . . If it increases inordinately therefore, it is because that state on which it depends has itself excessively expanded: it is because society, weak and disturbed, lets so many persons escape too completely from its influence.' Source: *Suicide* p. 373

For Durkheim the kind of society which has high rates of egoistic suicide is highly individualistic with each person looking out for his or her own interests.

Altruistic suicide – social solidarity high

'altruism . . . expresses . . . the state where the ego is not its own property, where it is blended with something which is not itself, where the goal of conduct is exterior to itself, that is, in one of the groups in which it participates. So we call the suicide caused by intense altruism, anomic suicide.' Source: *Suicide* p. 258

Altruistic suicide is the kind of suicide which people commit as an act of duty, because it is the correct thing to do in their society under the circumstances in which they find themselves.

Anomic suicide – social regulation low

'results from a man's activity lacking regulation and his consequential sufferings. By virtue of its origins we shall assign . . . the name of anomic suicide.' *Suicide* p.258

Durkheim's idea of 'anomie' expresses either the state of a whole society where morals and guidelines for conduct have become unclear (in conditions of rapid social change for example), or the state of an individual whose relationship to society is suddenly changed: a migrant from one society to another: a rich person suddenly made poor, or a poor person suddenly rich.

Fatalistic suicide – social regulation high

'is the suicide deriving from excessive regulation, that of persons with futures pitilessly blocked and passions violently checked by oppressive discipline.' Source: *Suicide* p. 276

The examples usually given refer to prisoners and slaves.

The unscientific quality of Durkheim's theory

Activity 8 will have shown you that without knowing the intention of the deceased, it is impossible to use Durkheim's classification of suicide. But there are more problems with Durkheim's theory.

To be scientific a theory must be capable of being proved wrong. The theory 'our lives are controlled by undetectable forces' cannot be scientific because there is no conceivable way of proving the non-existence of undetectable forces. Durkheim's theory of suicide goes something like this:

> Suicide rates reflect the kind and degree of social control in a society. High levels of social control cause altruistic and/or fatalistic suicide. Low levels of social control cause egoistic and/or anomic suicide.

This is a theory which could never be proved wrong by any conceivable test. Take the example of war. 'Great social disturbances and great popular wars rouse collective sentiments, stimulate partisan spirit and patriotism, political and national faith, alike, and concentrating activity towards a single end, at least temporarily cause a stronger integration of society.' (*Suicide*, p. 208)

In England and Wales suicide rates fell during war time, but in some other societies war has scarcely affected the suicide rate at all. Could this disprove Durkheim's theory that suicide rates are linked to degrees and kinds of social control?

No, because faced with *no change* in the suicide rate during wartime it could be argued that:

either	**or**	**or**
the circumstances of war had not altered the kinds and degrees of social control – hence the suicide rate remains the same and Durkheim's theory is saved	the circumstances of war had altered the kinds and degrees of social control, but in such a way that decreases in altruism (fewer altruistic suicides) were balanced out by increases in egoism and/or anomie (more anomic and egoistic suicides) and Durkheim's theory is saved	the circumstances of war had altered the kinds and degrees of social control, but in such a way that increases in altruism (more altruistic suicides) were balanced out by decreases in egoism and anomie (fewer egoistic or anomic suicides) and Durkheim's theory is saved.

Since Durkheim offers us no guidance on how to recognise different types of suicide when we see them, there is no way of choosing between these explanations. Whichever we choose supports Durkheim's theory.

In short then, Durkheim's theory is written such that no kind of evidence can disprove it. It is a having-your-cake-and-eating-it, heads you lose, tails I win, kind of theory. As such it is unscientific and doesn't explain anything very much at all.

ACTIVITY 9
Briefly explain the irony in the cartoon in the light of the above discussion.

9.11

If the anomie don't get yer the altruism will!

ACTIVITY 10
Using data 9.12 and 9.13, give the two kinds of reasons why suicide rates vary from society to society.

9.12

Suicide dies the death by Dublin decree

From Joe Joyce
in Dublin

Suicide has been officially abolished in the Irish Republic — not because people have stopped taking their own lives, but because coroners are forbidden to say that they did.

A decision by the High Court in Dublin last April means that verdicts of suicide cannot be brought in by coroners. As a result, the Republic has officially had a nil suicide rate since then.

This situation came about when relatives of a person recorded as having committed suicide challenged the coroner's verdict. The law has always prevented coroners from apportioning blame: verdicts on road accident victims, for example, could not say who was to blame.

The High Court ruled that this prohibition extended to suicide: coroners could not blame victims for their own deaths either.

Source: *The Guardian* 4.11.85

9.13

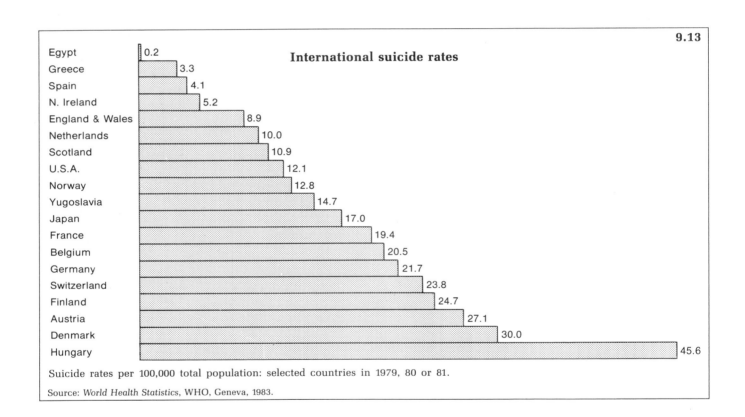

International suicide rates

Country	Rate
Egypt	0.2
Greece	3.3
Spain	4.1
N. Ireland	5.2
England & Wales	8.9
Netherlands	10.0
Scotland	10.9
U.S.A.	12.1
Norway	12.8
Yugoslavia	14.7
Japan	17.0
France	19.4
Belgium	20.5
Germany	21.7
Switzerland	23.8
Finland	24.7
Austria	27.1
Denmark	30.0
Hungary	45.6

Suicide rates per 100,000 total population: selected countries in 1979, 80 or 81.

Source: *World Health Statistics*, WHO, Geneva, 1983.

ACTIVITY 11
Data 9.14 contains extracts from interviews with two coroners plus details of five cases of death. Read the interviews and then decide which of the cases each of the coroners would give a suicide verdict to.

9.14

1. Female 35. Justice of the Peace. Car in high speed collision with motorway bridge. Weather good. No other cars involved. Car apparently in good mechanical order. Death happened on evening after being dismissed from her job for fraud, and having been told she would be prosecuted.

2. Male 18. Drowned after setting to sea in small boat stolen from its moorings. Sea calm and boat found floating uncapsized. Post-mortem showed he had drunk equivalent of 4 pints of beer. Had recently learned that his A level results were too low to admit him to medical school. Father and older brother are doctors.

3. Male 27. Mental patient. Died after swallowing small pieces of broken glass over a period of weeks. Had long history of swallowing objects.

4. Male, 63. Farmer. Died by hanging. Was given to melodramatic gestures; suicide notes and threats to kill himself with noose hanging in barn. Strangulation occurred after manger on which he had been standing collapsed. Death followed series of family rows over farm management. Left suicide note.

5. Female 58. Long history of depressive illness and alcoholism. Inmate of hostel for mentally ill. Had recently ended love affair with another inmate and had declared intention to kill herself. Had disappeared from the hostel and returned very drunk. Died from overdose of sleeping tablets. It was established that the tablets had been hoarded by her lover for whom they had been prescribed.

Coroner 1

There are some exceptions of course, but I think generally suicide is a symptom of a thoroughly disordered life. Suicide is usually only one critical and fatal incident in a whole pattern of self-destructive behaviour. The same people are often destroying themselves physically by drinking or self-neglect, and socially by the way they behave to other people.

When you look into it you usually find that it is triggered off by something which has upset the individual's equilibrium. It could be a sudden change for the worse, although not always. I understand that it sometimes happens with pools winners. I read that somewhere. Or it could be when someone realises that all their hopes and dreams are going to come to nothing.

Coroner 2

I understand that some coroners are somewhat cavalier with regard to the precise legal definition of suicide, and will bring in verdicts on very impressionistic evidence. But for me it is absolutely important to establish two things 'beyond reasonable doubt' as the law says. Firstly I want to be sure that the deceased intended to kill himself. Secondly that he actually knew that what he was doing would lead to his death. Unless you can establish both of these you shouldn't really bring in a verdict of suicide. You should use the 'open verdict' or one of 'misadventure'.

Back to the patterns

Your probable answers to Activity 10 were:

(i) that suicide rates vary from country to country because social circumstances in different countries are more or less likely to cause people to commit suicide.

(ii) that suicide rates vary from country to country because different societies have different ways of classifying and recording deaths.

The news story about Irish coroners (9.12) should have sensitised you to the fact that suicide statistics are not records of the number of people who intentionally kill themselves, but are records of verdicts about the cause of death. Activity 11 will have suggested that which deaths get classified as suicide has a lot to do with the ideas of the coroner who makes the decisions.

If suicide statistics are a record of the number of people who intentionally kill themselves	If suicide statistics are a record of verdicts about the causes of death
THEN	THEN
patterns in the statistics will reflect something about the reasons why people kill themselves.	patterns in the statistics will reflect the way in which decisions are made about the classification of deaths.

BUT

ACTIVITY 12

(a)   The study by Atkinson, Kessall and Dalgaard (data 9.15) is a good example of scientific method in use. Draw up a diagram showing how it conforms to the hypothetico-deductive method (see data 9.8).

Note that Durkheim operationalised suicide as an intended self-killing. Atkinson and his colleagues operationalised suicide as a death legally defined as such.

ACTIVITY 13

Using what you have learned already, write an essay showing how Durkheim failed to produce a scientific theory of suicide. You will need to make and illustrate the following points:

(i)   His categories of suicide are not operationalisable: it is impossible to apply them to any particular case.

(ii)   His theory is formulated in such a way that it would be impossible to prove it wrong. Thus it cannot be a scientific theory.

(iii)   He treated suicide statistics as counts of self-homicides and failed to see how the patterns in the statistics might derive from the ideas of people classifying deaths.

(iv)   However when suicide statistics are viewed for what they are – records of verdicts – it is possible to study them scientifically.

9.15

Danish vs. English coroners

Suspicious that suicide rates were the creation of coroners' judgements, W. M. Atkinson, Neill Kessall and J. B. Dalgaard investigated decision-making about suicide in England and Denmark. Four English Coroners and five of their Danish counterparts were asked to decide on 40 cases.

The Danes were much more likely to reach a suicide verdict than were the English coroners. The authors attribute this to the fact that in Denmark the verdict can be used when 'on balance of probability' suicide seems likely, whereas in England coroners have to find evidence of 'definite suicidal intention'. They argue that the consistently higher suicide rate in Denmark compared to England is due to the different rules for reaching a verdict, rather than due to people in Denmark being more likely to take their own lives.

Verdicts of five Danish kredslaege and four English coroners on the same 40 case records

	Denmark					England			
Suicide	32	31	28	27	27	23	21	17	16
Accident	6	5	8	12	6	9	8	10	13
Open	2	3	3	0	6	6	11	13	11
Natural causes	0	1	1	1	1	2	0	0	0

For differences between Danish/English suicide verdicts:
English mean = 19·25; Danish mean = 29.0.
$t = 5·21$; $df = 7$; $P < ·01$.

Source: Atkinson, W. M., Kessel. N. and Dalgaard, J. 1975 'The Comparability of Suicide Rates' *British Journal of Psychiatry* 127, pp. 247–56

Suicide stories

A suicide is a story told about a death: a story of how and why someone killed themselves. Everyone has ideas about why people kill themselves and they use these ideas to decide whether a death is a suicide or not.

Ordinary people, policemen, coroners, witnesses, juries and people in the media often turn a suicide into a moral tale to illustrate how something is so bad, that it causes people to kill themselves.

ACTIVITY 14

(a)   With the help of data 9.16 describe how common ideas abut suicide are recycled in society.

(b)   Using data 9.17 to 9.19, describe how deaths defined as suicide are pressed into service to make moral points.

(c)   Briefly suggest how the concerns and morality of the times influence whether or not a death is defined as suicide.

(d)   An 'A' level student dies and there is a verdict of suicide. Write two brief news stories one showing how intolerable examination pressure drives people to death, the other how young people today lack the moral fibre to cope with hard work and competition.

9.16

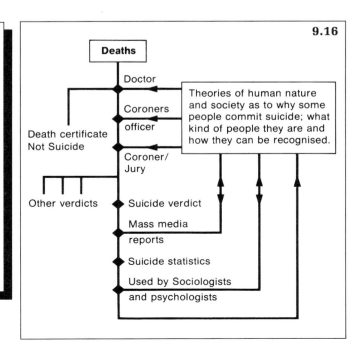

9.17

NO HOPE ON THE DOLE

NO WORK AND NOTHING TO LIVE FOR

Teenagers Mark and Daren had no jobs and no hope. So they killed themselves. Distraught parents found their bodies in a car in a locked garage at Daren's home only hours after returning from a celebration party . . .

Source: adapted from a *Daily Mirror* article

9.19

Retired coroner

During the War it was something of an understanding that you didn't bring in suicide verdicts unless you really had to. 'Bad for National Morale' – and of course I think most people felt responsible for keeping morale up. I think with suicide at that time we felt it was a kind of 'defeatism', defeatism in the face of the enemy, and that was a cardinal sin, letting the side down, you know. So when there *was* a verdict of suicide lots of coroners couldn't resist reading a sermon about moral cowardice. I expect I did.

9.18

'The Drunkard's Children'

In the 19th century alcoholism was seen as a major cause of suicide, not merely for alcoholics but for members of their families. Pictures and stories of suicide associated with alcoholism were especially common in the literature of the anti-drink, Temperance Movement.

The struggle to define the truth

Establishing a death as a suicide often involves people who would prefer one verdict rather than another. For the relatives and friends a suicidal death may serve as evidence that they neglected or pressurised the deceased. Doctors sometimes admit to destroying suicide notes because an inquest would be bad for the health of the surviving family. For prisons and mental hospitals, suicides are bad news, but not such bad news as homicides.

ACTIVITY 15

(a) Why would the South African Police be concerned to define Steve Biko's death as suicide?

(b) Go back to data 9.14. Take one of the cases and provide a fuller description of the circumstances and personality of the deceased:

   (i) in such a way as to suggest a verdict of suicide,

   (ii) in such a way as to suggest a verdict of accidental death.

9.20

Steve Biko

South African Black activist Steve Biko died after falling from a high window at Police Headquarters. While the official verdict was suicide, many people believe that he was murdered.

Actuality and artifact

Any set of social statistics confronts us with a puzzle. Do they show what they appear to represent – are they *actualities*? For example, do statistics on suicide actually represent self-inflicted death? Or, are social statistics simply a reflection of the ways in which information is collected and classified – are they artifacts? For example, do statistics on suicide simply represent coroners' definitions of suicide?

Both artifacts and actuality will show as patterns in statistics, but what is their relative contribution? With suicide we can be fairly sure that the statistics are a better record of reporting, investigating and coming to a conclusion about deaths, than about the social causes of death. This is inevitable because the definition of a suicide requires knowledge of the intention of the deceased and intention is impossible to pin down. Given this, it would be unwise to assume that patterns in suicide statistics indicate the social circumstances which cause people to kill themselves.

Further reading

Atkinson, J. M. 'Societal Reactions to Suicide' in Cohen, S. (ed) *Images of Deviance* Penguin, Harmondsworth, 1971
Atkinson, J. M. *Discovering Suicide* Macmillan, London, 1978
Cicourel, A. *Method and Measurement in Sociology* Free Press, New York, 1964
Douglas, J. *The Social Meanings of Suicide* Princetown University Press, 1967
Durkheim, E. *Suicide: a study in Sociology* trans. Spaulding J. and Simpson G., Routledge & Kegan Paul, London, 1952

Unit 10 The Social Construction of AIDS

Why is AIDS perceived as a social problem? This unit addresses the question with reference in particular to the role of the media in the construction of AIDS as a social problem.

Introduction

'Whenever people begin to say, "Isn't it awful! Why don't they do something about it?" we have a social problem.' From its initial identification in the USA in 1981, AIDS has developed into a complex social problem. 'It is not', as Vass points out, 'just the issue of health and illness (thus the medical condition per se)' which 'has captured the imagination of the public causing them to say Isn't it awful! and to ask for something to be done about it to stop the social problem'. In stark contrast cancer which has claimed many more lives than AIDS is not deemed to be a social problem, 'but remains in the minds of the people, an unfortunate undesirable personal trauma' strictly a medical problem. AIDS on the other hand involves a 'value judgement', a moral evaluation 'of the condition or its definition as bad'. (quotes from Vass, 1986)

Section 1 AIDS as a social problem

ACTIVITY 1

(a) Why are there no Cancer T-shirts or jokes?

(b) Vass points out that AIDS in contrast to cancer 'originates in social relationships'. What does he mean? In what sense is the capacity to make fun out of AIDS related to the way these social relationships are perceived?

(c) How do advertisements for AIDS T-shirts and AIDS jokes influence perceptions of AIDS?

10.1

'Have you got hearing aids?'

Source: Strip AIDS, Willyprods/Small Time Ink, 1987

K. Plummer (1985) distinguishes between two dominant ways of viewing AIDS – the Medical Model and the Stigma Model.

	Medical Model	Stigma Model
Focus:	Body	Behaviour/Life Style
Conceptualisation:	Scientific	Moral
Explanation:	Virus	Sin, Choice, Responsibility
Management:	Clinical	Segregation
	Therapeutic	Discrimination

Read the following extracts bearing this distinction in mind.

ACTIVITY 2

(a) Which extracts may be subsumed under the Medical Model and which under the Stigma model?

(b) What assumptions about homosexuality are made in data 10.2. (ii) and (v)? How does Drabble seek to justify his attitude towards gays?

(c) Drabble views myxamatosis – a disease which kills rabbits – 'as a natural control of overpopulation'. What point is he making by comparing this with AIDS?

(Comment on Anderton quote from Steve Bell in *The Guardian*)

10.2

Views on AIDS

(i) 'If AIDS is not an act of God with consequences just as frightful as fire and brimstone, then just what the hell is it?' (John Junor – Editor, *Sunday Express*)

(ii) 'AIDS horrifies not only because of the prognosis for its victims. The infection, origins and means of propagation incite repugnance moral and physical of promiscuous male homosexuality which, tolerable in private circumstances, has, with the advent of gay liberation, become advertised even glorified as acceptable conduct, even a proud badge for public men to wear.' (*Times* Editorial, 21.10.84)

(iii) 'AIDS is a condition which causes the body's immune system to collapse, leaving it susceptible to infection by often rare ailments...' (Vass, 1986)

(iv) 'Transmission occurs largely by sexual contact, especially homosexual, and by blood-to-blood inoculation. The risk of infection by blood inoculation is greatest through the sharing of needles and syringes among intravenous drug abusers...' (*Lancet*, 1985)

(v) 'The most sinister decline in our standards of behaviour is the tolerance of unnatural sexual behaviour. (Drabble is referring to homosexuality.) 'But the laws of nature are not so easily bent because the consequences of such observation is the current invasion of AIDS. It is a "plague" in every way as dangerous and as certainly fatal as myxomatosis...' and is 'spreading as inevitably as myxomatosis, not as a natural control of overpopulation but as the result of the unnatural practice of our artificially permissive society'. (P. Drabble, *The Field*, March 1987)

(vi) 'AIDS victims swirl in a cesspit of their own making'. (James Anderton, Chief Constable of Manchester)

The social reaction towards AIDS which seeks scapegoats has historical precedents in the social reaction to diseases such as the Black Death or last century's cholera pandemics for which Jews and the 'great unwashed' were respectively blamed. The Papal Bull of 1348 described the Black Death as the 'pestilence with which God is afflicting...' The following extracts explore the 'scapegoating' associated with AIDS.

ACTIVITY 3

(a) Why do the groups with whom AIDS has been most associated make ideal scapegoats?

(b) On the basis of data 10.3 (ii) and (iii) do you think the Black Death and cholera were perceived as *social* problems? Give reasons for your answer.

(c) What similarities do you note between Drabble's explanation of AIDS (10.2 v) and the explanation of cholera (10.3 iii)? Using the medical model, how might the high incidence of cholera among the 'lumpenproletarian scum' (the lower working class) be explained?

(d) During the Plague of London in 1665 'a red cross and the words "May God have mercy on us" marked the houses of plague victims forcibly imprisoned'.
(Gregg, *New Internationalist*, March 1987).

What sort of proposals might those who adopt the stigma model suggest to combat AIDS?

(e) Data 10.4 is an extract from proposals put forward by the Terrence Higgins Trust (Britain's main support group for people with AIDS) for curbing the spread of AIDS. What model of AIDS underlies these proposals – social stigma or medical? The proposals have not been given in full since the language might be considered 'unsuitable' for publication in a sociology text. Which would you find more offensive – The Terrence Higgins Trust proposals in full or the extract from the *Times* editorial 10.2 (ii) and why? Which do you think would generate more fear and emotion and why?

(f) How does data 10.5 challenge the social stigma model?

10.3

Looking for scapegoats

(i) 'Attitudes towards AIDS, and the tardy (sluggish, late) political reaction, have been shaped by the fact that from its first identification in the USA in 1981 it has been strongly associated with marginalised, oppressed or feared groups; with Haitians and subsequently with black Americans (a disproportionate number of American victims are black); with intravenous drug abusers; and with male homosexuals. AIDS has fed easily into wider anxieties and fears that find a focus in powerful streams of racism and homophobia (fear of homosexuals). The result has been predictable and disastrous: a "moral panic" rooted in a genuine fear of the disease, but seeking scapegoats in those who were the chief sufferers from it.' (J. Weeks, *Marxism Today*, January, 1987)

(ii) 'The ideal scapegoat should be: a) different, b) unpopular, and c) relatively defenceless. Lepers fitted the bill nicely during the Black Death, but they were unsatisfactorily few in numbers. Jews, however were everywhere, and in quantity. In the French province of Languedoc, three separate prejudices were blended ingeniously into an unholy trinity, and blamed for the Black Death. Lepers were accused of poisoning the wells (the usual allegation), after being bribed by the Jews who, in turn, were paid by the king of Grenada. This bizarre idea (and variants elsewhere) led to the slaughter of Jews throughout Europe.' (C. Gregg, *New Internationalist*, March 1987)

(iii) 'Arising from the degraded depths of Asia and then when sweeping across Europe, striking down the lumpenproletarian scum, Cholera was, in the eyes of many official spokesmen, nature's way of demonstrating that the "great unwashed" were intrinsically polluted and diseased.' (R. Porter, *New Society*, 12.12.86)

10.4

If you intend to stay with a single long-standing partner for ever more . . . fine. If you don't, or think you might not then Aids should be a matter of personal concern. To protect yourself and your partner(s) follow these simple guidelines.

If you're a man, **DO** wear a condom,

It can take time getting used to condoms.

DO experiment. find your favourite brand. and use plenty of water-based lubricant like KY.

The virus is carried in spunk or vaginal fluid. During oral sex you should avoid swallowing. The virus could be transmitted through cuts in your gums.

SEX IS GOOD. IT'S FUN.
IT'S UP TO ALL OF US NOT TO SPOIL IT.

Source: Terence Higgins Trust proposals (abridged version) from *Marxism Today*, March 1987

10.5

Source: *Strip AIDS*, 1987

Section 2 The role of the mass media in the construction of AIDS as a social problem

The media play a key role in shaping perceptions about AIDS, partly because it is the only source of knowledge, for most people, about AIDS. The media as S. Hall puts it 'do not simply and transparently report events which are naturally newsworthy in themselves' but construct images of social reality by setting the agenda i.e. by identifying the important issues to think and talk about and providing a general framework within which the discussion takes place.

ACTIVITY 4

(a) Data 10.6 is about a boy who contracted AIDS through a blood transfusion. Data 10.7 is about a woman who contracted AIDS through a blood transfusion and unknowingly passed it on during pregnancy to three of her children (the child in the photograph having developed the full-blown version of the disease) and during sex to her husband. In describing such sufferers as 'innocent' or having contracted AIDS 'through no fault of their own' what is being implied about people with AIDS who have not contracted AIDS by these means? How does the photograph from the *Sun* (10.7) reinforce the 'innocence' of the AIDS sufferers?

(b) Photograph 10.8 shows a gay person with AIDS being comforted by his lover. What sort of feelings does it invoke? Why do the sentiments conveyed by this photograph not fit in with the agenda set by the Sun?

(c) Photograph 10.8 was taken from a feature on AIDS in *New Internationalist*. Whose 'side' do you think the writer took – the side of gays or the side of those who condemn them?

10.6

Banned from school

13 year old Ryan White does a paper round every morning – wanders freely through his home town but isn't allowed to go to school because through no fault of his own Ryan has AIDS. In New York alone there are an estimated 150 children suffering from AIDS most of them infected while still in the womb, innocent victims who in many cases caught the disease because their mothers were drug addicts.

Source: Bob Friend, B.B.C.

10.7

By JACKIE MACPHERSON and NIGEL FREEDMAN

THE anguished mother who may have doomed her family to die of AIDS sobbed last night: "I look at them around me and wonder, My God, what have I done?"

Irene Raymond shuddered to recall the moment last October when doctors revealed the awful truth— through no fault of her own she had infected her three lovely daughters and her husband with the killer virus.

"It's hard to take in the full horror of what has happened to us," said 27-year-old Irene. "The situation is so enormous."

"I know it's not my fault but I can't help feeling I've condemned us all to death."

The loving mum was given AIDS-infected blood shortly after the birth of her first child Stuart.

So brave . . . Richard, Irene and tragic Claire

Source: The Sun, 18.7.87

10.8

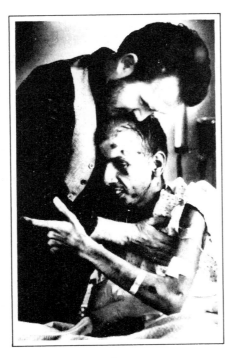

Source: *New Internationalist*, March 1987

ACTIVITY 5

(a) What evidence is contained in data 10.9 and 10.10 which suggests that the social stigma model set the agenda for Rock Hudson's death?

(b) How does this kind of reporting reinforce conventional moral values?

(c) Write a short newspaper article about Hudson's illness or death which does *not* give priority to the revelation that he was a life-long homosexual.

The last days of Rock Hudson 10.9

He died a living skeleton and so ashamed. Rock Hudson, Hollywood's macho sex symbol who, unknown to his millions of women fans, was a secret homosexual, died yesterday of AIDS.

Source: Bamigboge and McKay, *Daily Mail*, 1985

Rock's announcement in June that he had AIDS shocked the world. Till then, fans had known nothing of his tortured private life – that he was an avowed homosexual who often turned to drink.

Source: *Daily Record*, 3.10.85

Rock Hudson ill with AIDS 10.10

From Christopher Reed
In San Francisco

The news that the film actor. Rock Hudson, is ill with Aids and has also been a lifelong homosexual has brought consternation to Hollywood where no star has ever publicly come out of the closet.

The announcement in Paris that Mr Hudson has had the disease for a year prompted several news reports of his homosexuality. The actor himself has never made any public acknowledgement.

Friends of Mr Hudson's in San Francisco,

where he was a frequent visitor to its gay discos and clubs, say that the actor, aged 59, had considered publicly acknowledging his homosexuality, but finally declined. "He learned his lesson well in Hollywood and decided to stick by the rules," Armisted Maupin, gay writer and friend of Mr Hudson's said.

"These rules state that if you keep quiet, everyone will lie about it for you. All Holly-

wood will know, but never the public." Hollywood's voluntary conspiracy of silence is now threatened by the ravages of Aids, with other famous entertainers expected to fall victim and the news leaking out. Some believe that it might be preferable for homosexual stars to break the long-standing code and let their sexual preferences become known in less distressing circumstances.

Source: *The Guardian*, 27.7.85

ACTIVITY 6

(a) Would you expect to read about proposals for safer sex beneath 'gay plague' headlines (data 10.12 and 10.13)? Give reasons for your answer.

(b) Vass suggests that 'the mass media are part of the process of creating a "collective conscience" that informs and unites at the same time'.

Against whom do 'gay plague' headlines unite individuals?

(c) What point is the cartoon (10.13) making?

10.11

"This kind of journalism makes me furious!"

Source: *Strip AIDS*, 1987

10.12

gay plague

Source: *Daily Record*, 18.2.85

10.13

If fear of future dangers leads to safer sex and thus minimizes AIDS deaths, it will have proved a most effective educator. What's dangerous about fear, however, is that it rarely comes neat, but is always manipulated and exploited.. when the tabloids scream about the gay plague the message which comes across is about the plague of gays.

Source: R. Porter 'Plague and Panic', *New Society*, 12.12.86

A changed agenda – 'everybody's nightmare'

Despite the availability (since 1981-82) of evidence which showed that AIDS was not confined to homo-sexual men, it was not until 1985 that the media set an agenda which presented AIDS as 'everybody's night-mare' a menace afflicting 'the general population (perhaps 'you' and 'me', innocent, normal heterosexual men or women)'. This, Vass argues, was because 'the "gay plague" was no longer a novelty' and this 'called for the injection of something new, exciting, sensational, dramatic and highly personal'. AIDS was personalised – 'a general concern about infection was transformed into a personal fear of contamination in the process of normal sexual encounters, or, in the extreme, in the process of casual ordinary day to day social relationships'. (quotes from Vass, 1986)

ACTIVITY 7

(a) Why are data 10.14 – 10.17 particularly news-worthy according to the agenda set in 1985?

(b) 'The panic about AIDS and the ailment itself have been constructed as presenting a con-tinuous but changing threat...' (Vass, 1986) Why does Vass use the word 'constructed'? What has changed?

10.14

Tragedy of the family struck down with AIDS

[Headline for newspaper article, data 10.7]

Source: *The Sun*, 18.7.87

10.15

Threat to vital kiss

THE kiss of life could be out for ambulancemen because of the fear of catching Aids.

Crews have been told by their union to use other methods, including one-way valves. This follows talks with the Health Department.

Their move follows a similar ban by firemen at the weekend.

The Navy yesterday declared there was no danger of Aids on board HMS Liverpool, which recently visited Haiti, where the disease is rife.

Unions at Rosyth, Fife, where the Liverpool will berth on Thursday, had asked for assurances.

Source: *Daily Record*, 19.2.85

10.16

Scots children may be at risk

[Report on contaminated blood supplies for haemophiliac children.]

Source: *Evening Times* (Scotland), 22.2.85.

10.17

[A response to reports on parishioners refusing to take communion because of fear of contamination from chalices.]

Source: *Private Eye*, 3.4.87

The effect of transforming AIDS into a personal fear of contamination was to amplify panic. And while the new media agenda increased panic, it was itself reinforced by increased panic which tended to be reported in an uncritical and sensationalist way. A *Guardian* editorial (Feb. 1985) on news reporting of AIDS was entitled 'The real plague is panic'. When the media 'clears its throat the nation catches a cold. Or should it now be AIDS? No everyday human act, it seems, is too innocent to escape the menace...At the last count, you could catch it from sex, from blood transfusions, from infections, kissing, shaving, coughs and sneezes, swimming, drinking and even eating salads.'

ACTIVITY 8

There are only three ways the AIDS virus can be transmitted:

1) through sexual intercourse.
2) through direct blood to blood contact, and,
3) congenitally to infants born of infected mothers.

Bearing this in mind, write a short newspaper article on the QE2 incident. Comment on any differences between your article and the extract from *The People* (10.18).

10.18

Scandal of AIDS cover up on QE2

[The]...cover-up over the AIDS on board the QE2 is a disgrace...it highlights the fact that in spite of universal fear and ignorance about this horrific virus, AIDS is not a notifiable disease. At present any sufferer can and occasionally does discharge himself from hospital – and there is nothing doctors can do about it...That must not be allowed to continue.

[A report on the fact that passengers on the QE2 were not informed that a person who had contracted AIDS was on board.]

Source: *The People*, 1985

ACTIVITY 9

(a) In *New Society* (12.12.86) Roy Porter suggested that 'what is specially worrying...is that public denials (in fact AIDS is not casually contagious) all too often seem merely to fix the disinformation in the public mind (it must be true; why else are they denying it so fiercely)'. What disinformation might the highly publicised 'historic handshake' fix in the public mind?

(b) Even a proposed visit to a giraffe by a member of the Royal Family is newsworthy – see data 10.21. It was hardly surprising, therefore, that Princess Diana's visit to the AIDS Ward at the Middlesex Hospital received exhaustive media coverage. What evidence is there from the material from the *Daily Record* that it is Princess Diana rather than the plight of AIDS patients which is newsworthy?

(c) The *Daily Record* concludes that the visit of Princess Diana 'might help dispel some of the ignorance and prejudice', the 'historic handshake' putting 'paid to the myth' that it is possible to catch AIDS through social contact. Why is Princess Diana referred to as an 'angel' given the fact that AIDS can not be transmitted through body contact? What message does this convey?

(d) How might the visit and the way it was reported serve to reinforce negative sterotypes of gay people with AIDS? Refer in particular to the headlines and photographs and to the imagery of Princess Diana conveyed in these.

(e) What point is the cartoonist making (10.22)? How do you think he views Princess Diana's visit and the 'historic handshake'?

10.19

The 'historic handshake'

Diana shakes hands with an AIDS patient. 'She is absolutely charming,' the man told nurses later.

[caption from *Daily Record* 10.4.87]

10.20

Diana the angel of the AIDS ward
RECORD REPORTER

A DYING AIDS victim was photographed shaking hands with Princess Diana yesterday – at the Princess's personal request.

The 32-year-old homosexual was told the Princess felt a picture would explode the myth that AIDS can be caught by social contact.

CHARMING

The man later told nurses how delighted he was to meet the Princess. They spent several minutes chatting about his home life and the way the disease had affected him.

He told staff: "She was very sympathetic and seemed genuinely interested in how I was coping. she is absolutely charming."

The Princess had earlier shaken hands with the nine patients during her tour of the ward, and had spent 30 minutes chatting to them. She sat on the edge of their beds and frequently touched them as she talked.

"Her visit has gone a tremendously long way in calming people's fears about the spread of AIDS," said Professor Michael Adler, professor of medicine on the ward.

HYSTERIA

He added: "She was very concerned about the patients. The way she touched them and sat on their beds was very moving.

"She was very concerned about the hysteria that has been generated about AIDS. She was very positive in condemning the rather unfortunate situation we have seen in the way some AIDS sufferers are discriminted against."

Source: *Daily Record*, 10.4.87

10.21

IF I was a giraffe called Anne and I lived in the Marwell Zoological Park I confess I would have one dream – to meet my royal namesake, the hardworking and attractive Princess Anne. Well there is such a giraffe and this month she will meet the Princess. It will be a great day for one and all.

LONDONER'S
DIARY,
London Evening Standard

10.22

PRINCESS DI MAKES A VISIT

Source: *Strip Aids*, 1987

Who else could the media blame?

'With the growing recognition that AIDS is not a "gay disease" and can be transmitted heterosexually a new scapegoat became necessary. Women prostitutes apparently filled the bill nicely'. (Richardson, 1987). While women presented as sex objects help to sell tabloids, a woman who 'dares to exchange sex directly for money, rather than affection, security, housekeeping or a meal...meets with the full force of the classification "Whore"...a pariah set apart from the rest of society...labelled as stupid, immoral and depraved'. (Root, 1984)

ACTIVITY 10

(a) What 'unthinkable-for-me, pleasurable deviant act' (10.24) is being suggested in the cartoon (10.23)? Who is 'me' (with whom do you identify) the prostitute or a potential client? Does it simply depend on your sex? What enhances the 'additional pleasure of moral indignation' of the 'unthinkable-for-me pleasurable deviant act'?

(b) Why is it 'women as prostitutes and not their male clients who have been singled out as important in the heterosexual transmission' (Richardson, 1987) of the AIDS virus? Why do women prostitutes rather than their male customers make good scapegoats? What double-standard regarding male and female sexuality does this reflect?

(c) Does the passing of the Contagious Diseases Acts (10.25) reflect concern for the welfare and protection of women prostitutes or soldiers?

(d) The extract 'Speaking Out for Prostitute Women' (10.26) is a rare example of a scapegoat being given the opportunity in the media to articulate her view. What issues does she raise concerning prostitution, AIDS, women and sexuality by challenging the agenda which seeks scapegoats in prostitutes?

(e) Much more space was given in the magazine which carried Lopez-Jones's piece (5 pages compared to one sixth of a page) to a feature on a prostitute named only as Karen who was a drug addict and a person with AIDS. Do the extracts from this feature (10.27) confirm or challenge the agenda which seeks scapegoats in prostitutes and drug addicts?

10.23

DEATH FOR SALE

Forbidden pleasures

10.24

'There are many pleasurable feelings many people are forbidden to experience imagine, remember, dream about and they are definitely forbidden to talk about them.' (Laing, 1971). These pleasurable sensations that we have denied but not annihilated may be lived through again by means of the sensational newspaper. By reading a newspaper we are able to stumble across stories about the unthinkable-for-me, pleasureable deviant acts. We can read the details, be disturbed by the salaciousness of what is written, and then condemn what has taken place. We have thereby broken none of our...rules, and yet lived through the forbidden experiences and gained the additional pleasure of moral indignation.

Source: F. Pearce 'Mass Media and the Homosexual' in *The Manufacture of News*, Cohen S. and Young J. (eds), Constable, London, 1979, pp. 290-91

Contagious Diseases Acts

10.25

In the mid-19th century concern about the incidence of venereal disease among British soldiers led to the passing of the Contagious Diseases Acts. Under the terms of these Acts it was women suspected of being prostitutes, and not soldiers, who were required to register and have regular medical examinations.

Source: Richardson D. *Women and the AIDS Crisis*, Pandora, London, 1987, p.38

SPEAKING OUT FOR PROSTITUTE WOMEN

Nina Lopez-Jones

It's not true that prostitute women are a high-risk group for Aids. In fact, they take more precautions than most women. When your body is your business you have to be quite careful because if you're sick you won't be able to earn. Most prostitute women do ask men to use condoms. Some are now telling them to wear two, just to be extra safe, and anyone who doesn't like it can go elsewhere.

We are more concerned with the way Aids is being used to reinforce the old Victorian values that you should only have sex within marriage, and even then be careful because you don't know where *he's* been. Basically they are telling women: "Go back into the home and forget about your body being your own."

The media have gone ahead labelling prostitute women as high risk without any evidence. It has very serious implications. There was a woman in Soho who was stabbed to death a few months ago and a friend of hers said she thought it had something to do with Aids.

Source: *Sunday Times Magazine*, 21.6.87

10.26

Karen feels no guilt about the risk of passing on Aids to her clients: 'Why should I? They're all just dirty old men'

Karen works from Coburg Street in a dark and dispiriting part of town. Men drive along, take their pick of the girls, and the "lucky" one jumps into the car and they drive off. "We take them behind the General George carpet shop. There's a wall there and if you're behind that the cops can't see you."

It costs £20 a time. On a good night she'll pick up five or six in a quick succession. Of course she doesn't want to – she hates doing it; her boyfriend hates her doing it – but her habit costs £80 a day. "I used to do shoplifting, but I kept getting caught and fined. I've been down here for six years now, and I've only been caught once."

Karen lives in a council flat she shares with her boyfriend. It is on the 11th floor and is seedy through landlord disrepair rather than any neglect on her part. She and her boyfriend John – unemployed, also addicted, probably HIV positive – work hard at making it a home. The puppy, the hamster, the goldfish, a neat and clean kitchen, a scrubbed bathroom, ashtrays emptied as soon as they are used: dignity is maintained.

Yet within this little family there is intense love, unceasing concern. Even straight after a hit of heroin John took Nathalie gently for a bath while Karen cooked an evening meal. He worried about the lack of locks on the high windows, she helped Nathalie to feed the hamster. He tidied the toy box, she sorted the tiny socks into pairs.

Source: *Sunday Times Magazine*, 21.6.87

10.27

Yet more scapegoats

As the agenda switched from 'gay plague to heterosexual nightmare' not only women prostitutes but Africans became scapegoats – one of the most potent scapegoats a combination of the two, the African prostitute. 'A new "theory" which sought the roots of the AIDS problem in Africa, "the African Syndrome", displaced the original theory' which 'had led to the popular conception of the disease as a "gay plague". It introduced the public, via … medical information released and demystified by the media to the idea that AIDS was one more of those foreign, thus alien and mysterious enemies … a new form of "Black" Death … invading first the United States and the British Isles, and, gradually, the rest of the world.' (Vass, 1986)

ACTIVITY 11

(a) Write a list of ten words or phrases beginning with Black. How many have negative connotations?

(b) Bearing in mind McLurg's law (10.28 ii) and E.P. Thompson's observations (10.28 i), how might the news construct and affirm a racist world view? Think of examples of news reporting which reflect the operation of McLurg's law.

(c) Why does the 'African Syndrome' fit in so readily with the news values of the Western media.

(d) What policy proposals do you think the *Sunday Telegraph* advocated (10.28 iv)? How might these reinforce 'the symbolism of the race immigrant theme'?

Perceptions of blackness

10.28

(i) Writing about the Western media's perception of the Third World and the Western world E.P. Thompson (*Guardian* 18.4.86) suggests that 'wog blood' in the eyes of the media 'is of a different colour and quality to Western blood. This has been clear for several centuries. It is an inferior sort of stuff.'

(ii) Schlesinger in his study of BBC news points to the implicit adherence by news editors to McLurg's Law which delineates the newsworthiness of an event at home as against the newsworthiness of the same event occuring abroad. This law stipulates that 'one thousand wogs, fifty frogs and one Britain' are equivalent in terms of potential news value.

(iii) Writing about white perceptions of black immigrants in Britain, Hall et al (*Policing the Crisis*, 1977) stress the potency of the 'symbolism of the race immigrant theme, its capacity to set in motion the demons which haunt the collective subconscious of a superior race' triggering off 'images of sex, rape, primitivism, violence and excrement'.

(iv) In a few days time hundreds of students from Zambia, Uganda, and Tanzania will be arriving in this country. A significant proportion of them – possibly up to ten per cent – could be AIDS carriers.' (*Sunday Telegraph*, Opinion Column, 21.9.86)

ACTIVITY 12

(a) How might the social reaction to AIDS be described as a moral panic?

(b) With respect to AIDS what groups have been 'defined as a threat to societal values and interests' and by whom? Against what are 'right thinking people' 'manning the moral barricades'? Do people with AIDS feature among the 'right thinking people'?

(c) Hall *et al* (1977) argue that the news media assume the existence in society of a broad consensus of values, but, in fact, play a key role in constructing the impression of consensus by defining certain groups as 'folk devils' or threats to society. How? Answer with reference to reporting of AIDS.

(d) Write a paragraph explaining diagram 10.30.

10.29

Moral panics

Societies appear to be subject, every now and then, to periods of moral panic. A condition . . . or group of persons emerges to become defined as a threat to societal values and interests; its nature is presented in stylized and stereotypical fashion by the mass media; the moral barricades are manned by editors, bishops, politicians and other right-thinking people . . . Sometimes the panic passes over and is forgotten — at other times it has more serious and long-lasting repercussions and might produce such changes as those in legal and social policy or even in the way the society conceives itself.

Source: Cohen S. *Folk Devils and Moral Panics*, 1973, p.9

10.30

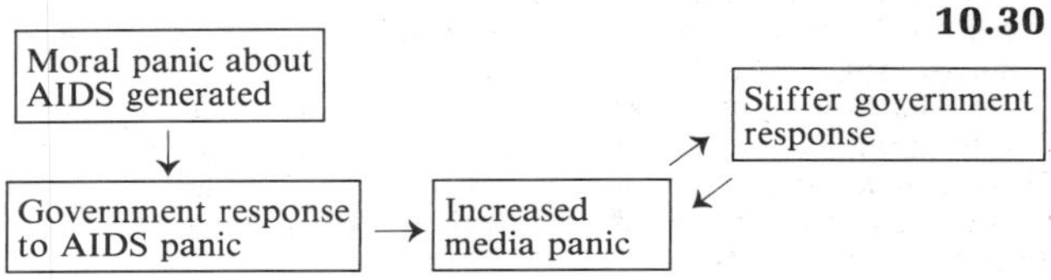

10.31

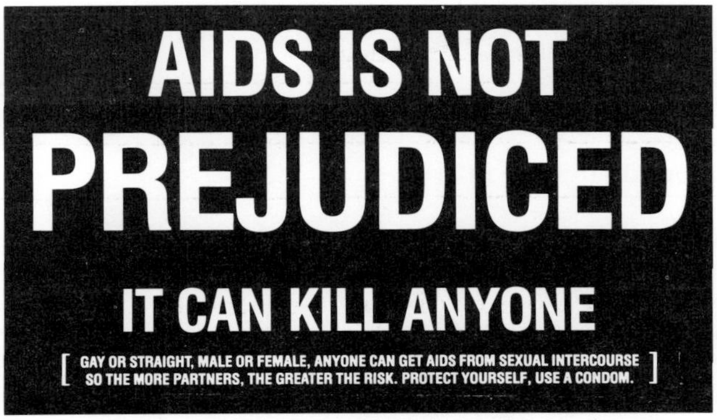

(From the Government's advertising campaign regarding AIDS.)

10.32

Jeffrey Weeks (*Marxism Today* Jan. 1987) argues that the formation of a Government body – the Whitelaw Committee – 1986, to deal specifically with AIDS was the result of AIDS 'ceasing to be a problem of troublesome minorities and being recognised as a problem for the whole of society'. This, in turn, resulted in a Government sponsored campaign to convey AIDS 'as a problem for the whole of society.'

Conclusion

AIDS is not simply a medical problem. It originates in social relationships about which moral judgements are made, and this has meant it has taken on the character of a social problem with social policy implications. What these implications are depends upon the kind of moral judgements made about the social relationships. AIDS does not immediately arrive as a social problem, but is constructed. Any account of the social problem of AIDS needs to examine its social construction, and since public 'knowledge' about AIDS is derived essentially from the media, this entails an analysis of the presentation of AIDS in the media.

The news media is not simply a mirror reflecting reality. Decisions have to be made about what counts as news and how it should be presented, and these reflect deep-seated moral values about social phenomena. In the presentation of AIDS these values dictate that certain sufferers are innocent and, by implication, others are guilty, (the 'innocence' of child and haemophiliac 'victims' indeed amplifying the culpability of the 'guilty'), that the 'guilty victims' are low in the 'hierarchy of credibility', in other words are unlikely to be given the opportunity in the media to speak for themselves, (unless as ashamed and pathetic figures), that sexual inclination is an issue of more gravity than the disease itself.

In the sense of setting a particular agenda for the coverage of AIDS, the media are constructing it as a social problem and providing a moral framework for the interpretation of it. Popular perceptions of AIDS changed not in response to new medical knowledge or the mutation of the virus, but because the 'gay plague' agenda was considered no longer newsworthy. AIDS became a problem for everyone – news stories and headlines focusing upon the potential danger of everyday activities of 'ordinary' people. The new agenda amplified panic about AIDS, for example, contributing to and being reinforced by fears of ambulancemen and firemen giving the kiss of life, fears of 'ordinary' businessmen and soldiers having 'ordinary' sex abroad, the Government's advertising campaign. Still there were the 'guilty victims', though added to gays were drug addicts, prostitutes and especially African prostitutes.

The social reaction to AIDS has taken the form of a 'moral panic'. Hall *et al* define moral panic as a displacement between 'threat and reaction, between what is perceived and what this is a perception of...created and orchestrated by police chiefs, politicians and most notably editors and journalists who perceive the threat in all but identical terms'. The effect of a moral panic is to construct (or reinforce) a sense of collective unity, common interest, national identity, of 'us' as against the perceived threat to 'us' posed by 'them' or in Cohen's terminology 'folk devils'. Thus we can speak of a moral panic about AIDS if the social reaction towards it consistently exaggerates the threat of it, sensationalizes it, and if certain groups of individuals are treated as the sources of the threat, 'depersonalised' ('implying that the individual is nothing but an instance of the discredited category') and cast in the role of 'folk devils'.

Further reading

On AIDS:
Altam, D. *AIDS and the New Puritanism* Pluto Press, 1986
Coxon, A. P. M. 'Towards a Sociology of AIDS' *Social Studies Review*, Vol. 3, No. 2
Porter, R. 'Plague and Panic' *New Society*, 12.12.86
Vass, A. *AIDS, A Plague In Us* Venus Academica, 1987

On the media:
Chibnall, S. *Law and Order News* Tavistock, 1987
Cohen, S. and Young J. *The Manufacture of News* Constable, 1981
Hall, S., *et al Policing the Crisis* Macmillan, 1978
Muncie, J. 'Much Ado About Nothing? The Sociology of Moral Panics' *Social Studies Review*, Vol. 3, No. 3

References

Unit 1

Barrett, M. and McIntosh, M. *The Anti-social Family* Verso, 1982
Berger, P.L. and Berger, B. *Sociology: A Biographical Approach* Penguin, 1976
Bowlby, J. *Childhood and the Growth of Love* Penguin, 1973
Ginsberg, S. 'Mothers in Employment' in *Women, Work and Conflict* ed. Fonda, N. and Moss, P. Brunel University Management Programme and Thomas Coram Research Unit, 1976
Laing, R.D. *The Politics of the Family* Penguin, 1971
Smith, D. *The Family, Marriage and Divorce* Longman, 1986
Tiger, L. and Fox, R. *The Imperial Animal* Paladin, 1974
Tolson, A. *The Family in a Permissive Society* CCCS, Birmingham University, undated
Wilmott, P. and Young M. *The Symmetrical Family* Penguin, 1973

Unit 10

Hall, S. *et al. Newsmaking and Crime* CCCS paper, University of Birmingham, Jan. 1975
Plummer, K. *Organizing AIDS* paper presented to the conference on 'Deviance and Social Policy', Middlesex Polytechnic, Oct. 1986.